UNDERCOVER JUNKIE
CHASING HIGHS, CONFRONTING KILLERS, AND UNRAVELING IN THE CHAOS

BRENT CARTWRIGHT

Copyright © 2024 by Brent Cartwright.

All rights reserved.

No part of this publication may be reproduced, distributed, or transmitted in any form or by any means, including photocopying, recording, or other electronic or mechanical methods, without the prior written permission of the publisher, except in the case of brief quotations embodied in critical reviews and certain other noncommercial uses permitted by copyright law.

This book is a work of creative nonfiction based on personal experiences. While it remains true to the essence of events, some scenes, dialogue, and details have been enhanced or altered for narrative purposes. Names and identifying characteristics of certain individuals have been changed to protect their privacy. All efforts have been made to preserve the emotional truth of these memories while respecting the privacy of those involved.

Published in association with Gatsby House:

www.gatsbyhouse.com

ISBN: 979-8-9921046-2-2 (ebook)

ISBN: 979-8-9921046-0-8 (paperback)

ISBN: 979-8-9921046-1-5 (hardback)

CONTENTS

Foreword	vii
Author's Note	ix
Prologue	1
1. The Real Brent Cartwright	11
2. Officer Cartwright	27
3. The Birth of Ricky	49
4. Stride	71
5. Super 8	89
6. Backpack	113
7. Junkie	121
8. Bud Ice	125
9. Jesus, Take the Meth	139
10. 726 Blackwood Drive	151
11. Let it Ride	167
12. Taco	193
13. Missing the Badge	215
14. Searching for Something More	227
15. July 15th	233
16. A Little Bit of Oxygen	253
17. Primal Panic	261
18. Recovery	275
About the Author	285

UNDERCOVER JUNKIE

FOREWORD

My first interaction with Brent Cartwright was confrontational. He glared at me as I opened my office door and motioned him in. Refusing to let me walk behind him down my office hallway, he passed through the open door, and I smiled as warmly as I could. Then, we awkwardly, non-verbally negotiated the hallway social norms for this situation. In the end, he limped down the hallway behind me, glaring at the back of my head, I'm sure. There was no mistaking the adversarial energy he brought to the first few months of our years-long engagement in treatment. He hated me and had no problem telling me so. Yet, this difficult dynamic would eventually transform into one of the most impactful relationships of my career.

Despite my credentials and experience with hundreds of cops continuously doing some of the most dangerous things imaginable, there has been no other more transformative career experience for me than uncovering what changed

Brent Cartwright. In all my years of training, I can confidently say that I have learned the most from my patients. And Brent is absolutely no exception. He had a front row seat to the greatest show on earth. So much so that he often became part of the show, not just the observer. He let me in on exactly what that experience was like, and now he will let you in on the same.

On the surface, this book is about wild rides, crazy experiences, and the stuff they make movies about. You can voyeuristically consume it as such, if you wish. However, the psychologist in me hopes you consume the content with more complexity. That you think about how we all can become junkies to the experiences of life, then engage in behaviors to avoid the numbness we inadvertently created. I bet if you think hard enough, you'll find the junkie in you too. The addiction most likely won't be to a substance, it will be to experiences that make you feel a certain way.

My hope is that *Undercover Junkie* will teach you about the human condition under extremes. That you will be humbled by the way someone can so quickly lose themselves in the pursuit of a goal, especially if they are convicted and strong-willed. But more than that, I hope you relate to his experience, even if you're not out fighting crime, but instead fighting emails, a growing to-do list, and challenging dynamics at work and home. The capacity to lose ourselves is in all of us. The willingness and tenacity to make the journey back to who you are is only in some.

—Jennifer Prohaska, Ph.D.

AUTHOR'S NOTE

As you dive into this book, I want to explain a few important things. What you're about to read is real. This isn't Hollywood. No one ever yelled, "Cut!" There were no directors; there were never any do-overs. In this line of work, mistakes can result in failed missions, serious injuries, or the death of a teammate or myself. For the sake of those still working these streets and to protect their identities, I've changed names, locations, and other details. The methods I used at work are still active today—both here in the U.S. and around the world. So, while I've shared the essence of my experiences, I've been careful not to disclose sensitive tactics, techniques, or classified equipment. If you're here looking for information on those specifics, you've grabbed the wrong book.

What I want to share with you is not just my life as an undercover detective—it's about identity, survival, and the silent struggles that no one sees. I spent 16 years as a police officer in a city that is a perennial top 10 most violent city in the U.S. The majority of my time was spent in the high-risk world of undercover narcotics. I faced dangers and challenges that, before this book, many could never imagine. I've endured both physical and emotional wounds, which eventually forced me to face something I had long ignored—the toll of living a life where truth and lies, and who I really am, became indistinguishable.

During my career, I became the very thing I was working so hard to stop. My undercover persona, which was once just a mask, became my reality. I lost myself in it. I became addicted to the adrenaline, to the constant rush of risk and chaos. Adrenaline is a dangerously addictive drug, and without even realizing, I did whatever was necessary to keep chasing it. In the end, it quietly eroded the person I really am. The toll of living multiple lives and hiding the truth from everyone around me was far heavier than I could have known.

My friends joke that, like a cat, I had nine lives—only I'd used up eleven of them. I laughed along, distancing myself from what really happened as if we were in a movie—a practice I came to know as depersonalization. The true problem was that those events—those close calls where I almost died—they were real. And they had lasting effects on me. That bill eventually came due. It wasn't until I was forced to leave the job that the weight of it all really hit home. The physical wounds eventually healed, but the scars from the stress, the loss of self-awareness and everything I barely lived through stayed with me.

I want you to understand that while my lived experiences are extreme, the impact of stress, burnout, and the sacrifice of self is not exclusive to those working in law enforcement or undercover roles. We all carry the weight of the work we do. It seems natural to find ways to compartmentalize, to hide parts of ourselves, but at some point, this takes a toll. And if we're not careful, our careers can change us in ways we never expected. To be blunt, there are consequences for total career commitment no matter what industry you are in.

This book is my attempt to make sense of it all. To share the truth of what it really means to live a life that is constantly at odds with who you truly are, and to shed light on the importance of staying grounded—no matter the world around you. I hope that by sharing my experiences, you can understand these dangers, but also the cost to the soul. The lessons I learned, often the hard way, are ones I hope will resonate with anyone who has ever struggled with the tension between their career and their identity. This is where I, like many others, got off course. Take my pitfalls as the glaring examples of what not to do.

In the end, we all need to find our way back to ourselves, before it's too late.

—Brent Cartwright

PROLOGUE
FUNNY FARM

Of all the shitty housing complexes in Kansas City, one of the most volatile scenes for meth addicts was a place the community referred to as the "Funny Farm." The location was off the beaten path and consisted of four apartments that had doors on all sides of the building, which drew crowds so devious that the place earned its name. The layout made it perfect for dope runners to mill back and forth without being caught with their stash on them. It didn't help that there were around forty people circulating at all hours of the day and night due to them being strung-out insomniacs, making it much harder to keep track of identities.

The shifty crowd who gravitated to The Farm became highly problematic for the surrounding neighborhood because they'd steal just about anything to fund their next high. Fights were constantly breaking out over money or disrespect. What would start as small altercations turned into droves of people almost bludgeoning each other to death, or dealers threatening to smoke suspect buyers in retaliation. Shootings and stabbings became more and more common in the area, which pulled me into play. When our squad approached our stable of informants, though, they were all immediately hesitant, saying the group was too crazy.

The consensus among our informants was that no amount of money was worth the risk, which was a good indication of how severe the situation actually was. Even a rumor that you were a snitch would bring a brutal ass-kicking. Finally, we got a new informant who was just dumb and greedy enough to help us out; so, being new together, I laid the usual ground rules with him. If he owed money or was screwing the dealer, we weren't going to go in for a buy. The last thing we wanted was to be put in a precarious situation because the informant was on rocky ground with dealers.

I circled The Farm with this informant to gauge the situation, as did my surveillance detectives. In truth, it didn't look good. There were around twenty gaunt, shadowy figures roaming the lot; too many to dodge or keep track of if all hell broke loose. The longer I stalled, the more anxious the informant became.

"Dude, if we're gonna go in, we gotta go in now—" he urged, "and you better not have anything worth a dollar in this fucking car. If we're gone too long, these fuckers will steal anything out of this shit box."

"Well—" I began, scanning the parking lot for a solution, "I'll solve that problem." I then veered the vehicle right next to an old man's apartment within feet of the door.

This made the informant inhale sharply as his jaw clenched and his hands balled into fists.

"Doug's not gonna like this," he said, wincing.

"You know, I don't really give a fuck what Doug likes," I retorted. "We're parking here. That's what's happening."

One thing I learned too late on the job was that cop instincts meant very little on the streets in this work capacity. Informants knew this world better than anyone, and it was best to at least entertain their advice. But my ego was too overpowering; nobody was going to tell me what to do.

According to the informant, Doug wasn't exactly a big dealer, but he was one of the major pushers at the complex. My plan was to hustle to the door and do the buy as quickly as possible. I tried to shift my attention from the sunburned junkies leering through the windows in the parking lot. It was evident right away that they hated my informant, and they were likely justified, given the annoying fuck I already perceived him to be. They hurled insults that were muffled by the windows as the informant and I steadied ourselves.

We opened our car doors at the same time and strode up to Doug's door without looking left or right. Two knocks and forty seconds later, the door opened to reveal a frail, greasy-haired man wearing jean shorts and no shirt or shoes. He turned from us more quickly than I'd anticipated and ordered, "Lock the fuckin' door." Normally, locking the door was something I tried to avoid; had I been the closest to the door, I would have fiddled with the handle and ensured the opposite, making sure my new "partner" and I weren't trapped in an execution scene that the SWAT team couldn't easily access. But the informant was behind me, so he, in fact, locked the door.

I sauntered behind Doug through the tiny apartment,

observing the six-by-six kitchen with no dishwasher, a small sink, and a mini-fridge. His dining room consisted of a folding card table and one chair. Everything was caked in filth. Because it was a studio, the bedroom was the living room. I eyed the rickety TV atop a crappy, wooden dinner stand. One high-back, floral chair from the seventies sat in the corner; it looked worn in, and, given the fact that the dude appeared to have no bed, I had to assume he slept there somehow (if he ever actually slept). This was common—someone who sold thousands of dollars of meth a week could have the worst living situation and nothing of value to their name. For a guy like Doug, government assistance provided food and shelter, but his dope profits funded his addiction.

We reached the living room and, with nowhere to sit, I stood and started the conversation, even though Doug didn't know me from shit. Mid-conversation, the informant caught me off guard by asking for a sale.

"Hey man," he interrupted, "we need fifty."

Doug shot an irritated look at my informant that I didn't initially question, mainly because I was irritated, too. I had explained the parameters of a deal to the fucker ad nauseam. He knew how this was supposed to go: I had the money, and I would set the deal. The informant proceeded to pad his pockets as Doug's glare seared holes through him. I broke his focus by pulling out my money and proceeding to wave it at Doug.

"Yeah, man—" I pressed. "I got fifty."

He took my money and held onto the meth, which was laid out on the table, glaring at the informant. "Now we're straight—you owed me, motherfucker."

As he stated this, a sharp ping of rage hit me in the top of the head. I shot the informant a glare.

This motherfucker, I seethed.

"What the fuck, man? That shit's between y'all!" I insisted.

His stare grew even more intense.

"The fuck you say to me?" Doug spat.

"Gimme my fifty back or gimme my goddamn shit!"

I glanced again at the informant, who was essentially pleading with his eyes by this point for us to go.

"C'mon, Doug, man, I told you, I'll get you your money. Can you just let it go this one time?"

As he pleaded, Doug began to work up his next hit. He pulled out a crusty syringe with a cockeyed, half-bent needle with no cap on it that had been nestled between cigarette butts and candy wrappers on the table. He then mixed his shit with some Visine, diverting his attention from the pleas of my informant who had become a cancer on this buy at this point.

"Hey, man, you're gonna have to give me my money or some shit," I stated flatly.

"That's not how this fucking works," Doug said, shifting to find a vein in the crook of his elbow. I waited until blood engulfed the tip of the stained needle, for his eyes to roll back into his head. Then, I quickly grabbed the baggie that he had taken out to mix his meth and stepped backward. The informant leaped back as Doug reached between the chair cushions, pulling out a gun. He sprang to his feet, arms and fingers outstretched, reaching for me. His eyes practically bulged out of his head as he lurched in my direction, ripping the baggie from my hands. I heard the needle hit the floor before I noticed the blood oozing out of his arm.

He pointed the gun at me, then at the informant, then back at me.

"Get the fuck out, motherfuckers!" he bellowed. He aimed the pistol in the informant's direction who was all but pissing down his legs.

"DON'T EVER COME BACK HERE AGAIN!"

Adrenaline rushed through me, which blocked any fear out of my system. I became more Ricky than I'd ever been: a cocky fuck who felt emboldened and far more in control than he actually was.

"You ain't gonna point that shit at me when you're the one who stole my fucking money!" I exclaimed. As the words left my mouth, all I could think was, *Fuck this, I can handle this guy. Doesn't he know who the fuck I am?*

Now, I was the crazed one. I stood with my feet apart, eyes wide and unblinking, fists clenched. I stared down the black barrel—a tiny tunnel of death—unflinching.

You don't get to take my money, motherfucker . . . the reel in my head played on.

Suddenly, I felt the informant's hand on my shoulder.

"Dude, Ricky, let's get out of here," he prodded.

My ear pricked up to the quiver of terror in his voice as he said my name. Only then did I realize the gravity of the situation that I had perpetuated.

Fuck. I knew I'd taken it too far.

"Fuck you, chicken shit pussy," I conceded.

The informant had already hastened to the door behind me; I could hear him fiddling with the squeaky knob. I proceeded to step backward, holding my breath, until I'd made it over the threshold of the apartment to the porch. There, I turned away from the apartment and slowly stepped towards my van. The informant was already waving away a crowd that had gathered to peer into my windows.

"Get the fuck off my shit," I bellowed, knowing the group was shuffling away gawking only because Doug was standing on the porch wielding a gun with blood gushing down his arm.

We jumped in and had hardly closed both doors before peeling out of the parking lot in a blur. I was both entirely disembodied and barking at the top of my lungs: "YOU STUPID FUCK. WHAT THE FUCK DID I SAY ABOUT OWING MONEY?"

"Dude, dude, dude—" my informant began, but was immediately interrupted by the crackling of my police radio.

"Hey, you guys, what happened?" my boss asked. In a condescending tone, I explained how Doug took my money and kicked us out of his place. My boss demanded we meet him in an abandoned parking lot to discuss this further.

"Ricky," my boss sniped, later. "Why did you let your money walk?"

"Well, he had a gun pointed at me—" I stated.

"You should have taken the dope!" he insisted.

"That's *why* he'd pointed the gun!" I argued. "I half expected him to shoot me in the fucking head." I explained, laughing it off as if I was detailing a scene from a movie and not real life.

"Okay, so go back and get your money. We don't let our money walk!" he insisted.

Still laughing, I fired back, "You're kidding, right?"

He was not. My boss was new and had never spent any time in this world, as a cop or before his career. It was crazy that I had to talk him out of forcing us to go back and knock on Doug's door. For the first time, I felt my judgment was questioned when it shouldn't have been. It is true that only *you* can really know what it's like in these buys. If my boss had any clue, he would not have argued at all. Instead, I was berated for losing fifty dollars. There was no concern over how I may have felt or how I reacted to having a gun at my head. But again, I showed no trepidation either.

It is hard to explain it really. In the moment, everything was totally numb. I stood facing that maniac and basically dared him to shoot me. It wasn't that I was oblivious to the severity of the harm I could receive. My mind was just blank, and I was on autopilot. I was just being Ricky.

I was pissed off at the informant and my boss. I wouldn't even be mad at myself as I was so blind to what I was doing. There was no seeing that I was to blame. I felt I was always right, and if something ended in a less-than-perfect way, someone else was to blame. I also got such a rush from the entire buy attempt that I was feeling energetic. I was hyper and ready to do something else that night. It was late and our night was over. So, I was destined to go to the office and complete some boring paperwork, which brought a terrible sense of an incomplete job...or the worst feeling ever. Failure.

Within an hour, I was still amped up and at home. While I stayed awake all night, my mind barely cooled from its overdrive state. This led me to play out hundreds of "what if" scenarios. All of these revolved around how I should have done things better during this buy attempt. Not a single thought about pissing off the dealer crossed my mind. They all played out on what I should have done once he pulled the gun on me. In my head, they all made sense and would have made a great movie scene. In real life, they would have gotten me killed. But I wouldn't believe that. I'd already proved I couldn't be killed. I always won, so I would just keep pushing the accelerator. That was my new normal. The only way I could operate.

CHAPTER 1
THE REAL BRENT CARTWRIGHT

"LET'S GO! LET'S GO! THROW THAT SHIT AWAY! YOU'RE MOVING ENTIRELY TOO SLOW!"

A drill sergeant with bulging eyes and a thick neck vein towered over me, spewing spit as he barked orders, watching as I awkwardly unzipped my bag, hesitated, then shook out the contents onto the floor, while I continued to worry that I'd left something in the stale pockets of my light-wash Levi jeans.

It was June of 1997, and I was an eager kid who'd just finished high school. I wanted to serve my country and community like my grandfathers who had fought in World War II, my dad who was in the Army in Vietnam, and my brother who signed up just after the first Gulf War. I had a bigger goal—to continue my education—but there was no way to afford it on minimum wage, and working construction didn't interest me anyway. I was a track star in school, able to physically push myself to the brink, pushing through a pounding heart and thick streams of sweat. I knew I could make it in the Army without question, and that was the best way to get a lot of money for college. So, I shaved my head to save myself from the Army barbers, signed up, and abandoned my town of two-hundred-some people in the rural outskirts of Kansas City for Lawton, Oklahoma, only two weeks after I crossed the stage in a cap and gown.

The other new recruits and I touched down on the thin landing strip outside Will Rogers Airport at about midnight and were bussed over to Ft. Sill, where we were assigned bunks and were now having out bags rifled through. I looked around at the other guys; my tiny town was as whitewashed as they come. And here I was, surrounded by men from all over the country—an array of colors, cultures, and socioeconomic backgrounds. The training base was a melting pot, and I wasn't sure how to act, where my place was, or what the actual fuck I was doing.

Everything we brought would be tossed out, except for pictures of girlfriends and parents, or small keepsakes that we could keep tucked away. The drill sergeants even went after hygiene products like cologne and mouthwash; apparently a dry campus could make people desperate, and guys would start drinking anything to catch a buzz. I looked around at the other trainees—at just eighteen, I looked like a clean-cut dork by comparison. Although there were a few other trainees as young as I was, they were few and far between. Most were older—in their twenties and a few in their thirties—and seemed hardened. Most of the guys in the bunks across from me looked like obvious criminals, then I learned they were from Florida and realized that was just how they looked.

I found out pretty quickly that personalities were strong in the military, and I wasn't like anybody else. Physically, I was scrawny—5'9" and 109 pounds—and, mentally, I was motivated. I had real plans for my life, wanting to give the military my all as a stepping stone to a bright future. Most other trainees were just there to earn a little "easy" cash or to get themselves out of trouble in some way—many of them were just looking for a way out of their hometown. I quickly learned that a lot of people join the military because they don't have any other prospects in life. Some want to play God and kill people, and very few give two fucks about anything.

Speed tests were a common part of character-building in the military. They only gave people a sliver of time, rendering the task at hand impossible, so they failed. The point was to reprogram shitty habits and turn trainees into soldiers. There was no beating the system—it wasn't in the cards. I realized early on that my real training was to tell Austin, a 250-pound street boxer from Tampa, that he needed to listen to my orders and polish the motherfucking sink. Of course, Austin had a criminal record, so directing him was like trying to move a boulder up a hill, but dismissing him meant getting my ass handed to me by the drill sergeant, and I wasn't going to let that happen.

So, there I was, in the Southwestern corner of Oklahoma, sweating out a hot-as-balls summer, enduring the most exhaustive training of my life, eating a surplus of 3,000 calories per day to make weight, falling in line, calling cadence, leading cadence, fucking up at leading cadence, and paying the price for my mistakes. Punishments were inevitable—whether a "mistake" was a true mistake, or an unavoidable misstep in a manufactured lesson, we were sent to the sandpits, and the entire group was punished.

"CARTWRIGHT! One of the stalls is missing a new roll of toilet paper! EVERYBODY! Get in the sand and beat your face!"

Our platoon would head down, in full uniform, sweating out muggy 100-degree days doing fucking flutter kicks. The sun was ruthless. We were forced to unroll our sleeves to protect our skin from the sun; the fabric didn't breathe, leaving us one exhale away from heatstroke. We exerted all of our energy and barely slept. At any given time, we'd wake up to the sound of chanting. Our assigned wake-up time was 4 a.m., but anyone who fucked up would be digging a sidewalk edging with a kitchen spoon, sweeping a parking lot the size of five football fields with a stiff bristle broom, or being yelled at by a drill sergeant before that.

Days were especially hard for me because I was selected for the Army cross country team, which demanded I wake up an hour earlier than everyone else and go on a six-to-eight-mile run followed by our usual PT session. I was also placed on a double-rations diet. "CARTWRIGHT! Ranger Diet for you!" I'd hear. When we'd go lap chow for breakfast, lunch, and dinner, I'd be required to stand at the front of the line with the other skinny dudes, and the drill sergeant would give our trays a once over.

"DOUBLE UP, MY GRANDMA IS BIGGER THAN YOU PUSSIES!" they'd yell. Then we'd pile on as many fats and proteins as we could load ourselves with. With only twelve minutes to eat, we'd break from getting food, head straight to our table, plop down, and shovel heaps into our mouths until we felt sick. Then, we had to check in with the drill sergeants to confirm we'd cleared our plates, right before we went to run laps in the blistering sun.

Once I put on some muscle, I started getting hungrier, housing food a bit better, and enjoying stuffing myself a little more. By five months into training, I'd put on sixty pounds of solid muscle—half of my body weight.

Halfway through basic training, the drill sergeants laid out what it would take to become the Distinguished Honor Graduate, and I immediately knew I wanted to work towards it. The accolade would be based on a cumulative evaluation. They'd look at our PT times, and we'd be evaluated three times per week on the skills and knowledge of everything we'd learned. We'd then go through an oral interview with the board and be required to carry out a skills demonstration where they'd put us in front of an M60 and watch us do a functions test, tear it apart, then rebuild the machine gun and shoot it. If someone became a Distinguished Honor Graduate, they'd be the "top soldier" throughout our entire five-month training.

I burned the candle at both ends all the way through testing, then kicked everybody's ass on evaluation day. The drills had become muscle memory—I only spoke handbook, and my scores showed it. The honor meant I would be recognized individually at graduation. My family would sit in their assigned seats, listening as my name was read, then a script about my accomplishments—all kinds of stupid shit aside from their announcement of my promotion. Being a Distinguished Honor Graduate meant I'd be promoted from Entry-Level Private, to Entry-Level 2 Private, to Private First Class. (Read: major dirtball, tolerable dirtball, and less of a dirtball.)

"Who is this kid?" my dad asked when my parents arrived for my graduation, slapping my back and giving me a firm hug. My dad was an awesome yet quiet and stern figure in our family, always pushing us so that our lives would be better in the future. He was one to acknowledge both my mistakes and accomplishments, though he wasn't overly emotional, so a hug was always unexpected. I'd changed a lot since Missouri. I'd always been a great son—respectful, smart, resourceful, driven, maybe a little too much of a class clown, though I kept my nose mostly clean—but aiming to be a soldier made me into a man and motivated me more than ever before.

By January of 1998, I'd become Army Pfc. Less-Of-A-Dirtball Cartwright, a small-town kid turned soldier, who'd accomplished what he'd set out to achieve. I was even rewarded with a letter of recommendation for West Point from my Captain. But I hadn't envisioned making the military my long-term career, so I tucked it away as memorabilia and forgot about it.

I'd joined the Army with the goal of funding college, not because I wanted to fuck with tanks. Instead, I wanted to find the path of least resistance; a way to serve without sacrificing parts of myself that I might never get back. So, I found my way into the National Guard where I could stay mostly free, and applied to the University of Missouri, which I got into the following semester.

College was a primer for my action-oriented self. My best friend and roommate, Alex McFarland, had a badass GSXR sportbike and showed crazy skill by riding a wheelie faster and longer than I'd ever seen. I bought my own GSXR and spent my nights with him and a bunch of others racing on back roads in excess of 130 mph. On nights that didn't end with someone wrecking and an ambulance hauling them off, we'd end up at the bar, drinking until we couldn't remember each other's names. Many nights, we'd find ourselves in fist fights, which gave me more broken hands than I can remember. Sometimes, our group would be hugely outnumbered; other times we'd "win" only to have to run just as the police arrived. I refused to back down from any challenge, even if it meant getting my ass kicked—which happened more times than I like to admit.

In October 2003, I was bid an early farewell with a "fuck you, Cartwright," from my National Guard Unit and reminded of a rarely mentioned code. This was a phrase given to us in case we were being deployed so we knew if it was real or a drill.

Then, at the end of the month, I got a call from one of the front office staff who tried his best to stay level-headed with me.

"Hey, Cartwright, it's Williams, what you up to?" the guy had the audacity to ask me.

"It's only been a month, you fucking idiot! What do you want?" I asked. His gravelly laugh told me all I needed to know: the joke was on me. He would go on to tell me that my unit was being activated and deployed. Since my actual ETS (Expiration of Term in Service) date was January 2004, I would be stop-lossed and sent with them.

Everything came to a grinding halt when I got that call. I'd been accepted to several law schools, was dating the woman who would eventually become my wife, Wesley, while simultaneously trying to choke down the fact that I had to go to the Middle East and see real combat. Wesley had just graduated from college, and we were in the process of planning where to move and which career paths to take, to which this devastatingly put a stop.

In 2003, the U.S. had only just started invading Iraq, though they'd been bombing the shit out of Afghanistan for the better part of two years. They needed military police: convoy security running supply lines. So, they sent my ass off to Ft. Leonard Wood to train me as a military cop, testing me every step of the way by designating me to an island of misfit toys who definitely didn't want to be reclassified to this job. I'm sure the military had their plans well in advance of any of this, but my unit just so happened to be chock-full of non-deployable soldiers: they didn't meet height or weight requirements, struggled with injuries, or had seedy shit in their background that prevented them from becoming police officers.

Half of the guys ended up having DWIs—an automatic disqualifier—and the other half had various criminal records, which would have been okay if they were going to be artillerymen, but not cops. Our unit ended up being in such bad shape that the Guard kicked almost all of them out and backfilled us with six other units.

Our *less* embarrassing group was sent to Ft. Leonard Wood to be retrained, and man, did some of us need it. They locked us down in old World War II barracks in Missouri, suffering alongside the alcoholics who were drying out while the rest of us went cold turkey on normalcy. Iraq couldn't kill us if we killed each other first—and it was possible, as we were at each other's throats constantly.

We trained through Christmas with no days off, and in February, we saw a major shift: most of us were raring to tear into the Middle East, shoot 'em up, and play the game. We were ready to grit our teeth, hoist packs on our backs, and place our boots on the rocky ground in the name of motherfucking freedom. Yet, things took a wild turn. The military must not have trusted us and decided to keep us stateside. Our excitement, which had taken so much time and effort to muster, was instantly squashed. My family was grateful I would be spared from combat, while I was on the opposite end of the spectrum. I was upset that I would miss out on my generation's great war.

———

Stationed in Ft. Lewis, Washington, I got my first taste of being a police officer. Remember, none of us wanted to be cops in the real world (which we still weren't, technically, we were only kind-of cops) and most of the guys I'd come in with had no wish to do this job. Our unit was mainly made up of farmers, mechanics, and truck drivers. I was doubly pissed: first, because I had to eat crow after flinging two middle fingers at everyone in the Guard I worked with (and thought I'd abandoned) when I turned in my gear, and second, because I'd done all this training to go overseas and was stuck in Washington.

While deployed, it also became abundantly clear to me that the soldiers were in desperate need of advocacy. The higher portions of our command staff definitely weren't doing it. The working conditions were trash, and right when we thought it couldn't get any worse, they pulled a third of our group to become prison guards—and I was one of them.

While some of the soldiers I worked with did a piss poor job to cope with our dismal circumstances (meaning they would do the bare minimum and create more work for everyone else), I tried to look at the whole thing as an opportunity to better myself. When I started working patrol, for example, I was never the type to just go through the motions. I took that shit seriously. When I was out, behind the wheel of a cop car, I'd proactively look for bad guys, and usually, I would find them.

One night, I was patrolling a secluded base parking lot when I spotted a guy shining a flashlight into the windows of parked cars. I rolled over and stopped, realizing the guy was a tweaker: skinny, covered in scabs, with dirt-caked fingernails. He told me his truck was in the lot, pointing to a beat-up Chevy pick-up with trash packed up to the ceiling inside;

he probably lived in it. I ran the plates and—as I'd suspected—learned the truck was stolen.

He's just some random shitbag that's trying to break into soldiers' cars, I thought, which enraged me, because a lot of these guys had just gotten home from Iraq. There wasn't much worse than a thief, in my opinion, and to steal from someone who just made it back from a year and a half of war—oh hell no. I got out of my car, assuming this would go the way most of my other arrests went: a compliant suspect and a quick drive back to the station for a report.

What began as a verbal argument between us escalated to my trying to latch him as he struggled to break free. Seconds into the fight, he pulled out a 25-caliber revolver, trying to point it at me to assist his escape. As the gun waved in his trembling hands, I lunged and took him down hard to the ground and fought to take the gun. While wrestling him on the pavement, my partner came running from behind a parked car. He had been inspecting the cars in the lot for signs of damage and, together, we disarmed the guy and got him in handcuffs. Once we were able to identify him, we found out that he was an Army deserter, strung out on meth as he escaped his unit's deployment overseas. After the night had come to a close, the two-star general that was in charge of our post found out about the incident and gave us an award and a write-up as a little "attaboy." Then, there were the less driven folks in my unit who would ridicule me, telling me this was what I got for not just finding a place to park and sleep my shift away.

Our platoon would soon be tasked with the role of guards at the prison located on the post. I would get the notice that I would be exempt from prison guard duty, as the deserter who tried to shoot me was housed in the facility. Therefore, I would be spared from this undesirable task, but as a group my platoon and I were pushed into an adjusted work schedule. We would now have to work over 80 hours per week with only one day off. This also led to us missing almost every meal, which was the one perk of military life that helped offset the low pay.

Having high self-efficacy, I chose to act, not only for my benefit but for all of us. There had to be a policy in place about this; getting a per diem for meals missed had to be in the regulations. So, I got to work, combing through the military's policies surrounding the matter, which did say that soldiers were allowed per diem if their schedules prevented them from eating during chow hall hours. When I approached my first sergeant and showed her the policy, she noted she'd take it to the colonel, but returned in a few days, saying it was denied, and no accommodations could be made.

"So, what are we supposed to do?" I asked.

"I don't know what to tell you. Deal with it," she responded.

She fucked with the wrong, motivated dude. I knew this was wrong, so I decided to write to my congressional representatives, then one letter became ten, and before I knew it, my efforts had become an extensive campaign. I exchanged correspondence with a family friend, who happened to be a colonel in the Department of Defense budget office at the Pentagon. Shit popped off fast after that. That same general who had given me an award just a few months before got a call from the budget office at the Pentagon, asking why soldiers weren't getting food. Around 6 p.m. that evening, in the middle of my shift, I received a command from my first sergeant.

"Cartwright, shift's over. Turn in your gear and come to my office."

I arrived at the office unaware of what was happening, but knowing it wasn't good for me if the first sergeant was still working at 6 p.m. Then, my platoon sergeant informed me that the provost marshal, a colonel who actually made all the post decisions, wanted to have a word with me.

I was led down the hallway by my captain, first sergeant, and platoon sergeant to the colonel's office. As my first sergeant stepped through the door, she immediately stiffened to salute him.

"Sir! Good evening, Sir! I've got Cartwright here as ordered, Sir."

I followed her lead by stepping inside. I saluted Colonel Swengross, then stood at attention, keeping my mouth sealed shut until he asked questions. He sat at his desk, mouth bent, arms folded in his crisp uniform, glaring holes into me through his reading glasses.

"Cartwright, I'll tell you right now, you're not in trouble," he began (though judging by his tone, I wasn't convinced). "Hell, you're allowed to write letters to anyone you want. But where THE FUCK do you get off—AND I MEAN WHERE THE FUCK DO YOU GET OFF? Why am I hearing about this bullshit from the fucking general and not your chain of command?" My pulse throbbed in my temples as he shot up out of his chair, pointing his finger in my direction.

Constricting every muscle in my body, I stood as still as possible, breathing through my nose.

The colonel tore my ass up for several hours—asking leading questions, verbally annihilating me, and shutting me down whenever I tried to answer—before finally letting me go.

Though my command staff refused to own up to what they didn't do, chow hall hours were—coincidentally—adjusted immediately. Over the following weeks, they experimented with mealtime policies. First, they provided coolers full of leftovers for overnight workers, but that was deemed unsustainable as the upkeep would be too much for the civilians who ran the kitchen. They settled on giving us "Jimmy Dean meal packs" (boxes of the vilest fucking food they could slap together): a bag of Ruffles potato chips, a small navy tin of Vienna sausages, and a little metal can of orange juice.

I was openly referred to as a "complainer" and "their problem child." But I was one of the hardest workers, and I took on what should've been their job of taking care of my tribe. The only payoff I got for taking a stand happened during the last leg of deployment, when our captain and first sergeant called our unit to attention, then stated that our work schedule had been pulled and evaluated.

"If you worked a day shift in the prison, or an overnight shift during certain months, you will be back paid $1,500 in per diem for the meals you purchased out of pocket," they said. But even after people were told they were getting back pay, it didn't erase my reputation as a disrupter. No, we'd never been in combat together, but I couldn't help but recognize the irony of it all. For a group of degenerates, I had made my life a fucking living hell. For a group of people, half of whom I couldn't even stand and who probably hated me even more, I had fallen on a grenade.

Once out of the Army for good, I realized I'd missed the deadline to reapply for law school. Now I had to wait another year and would soon lose my motivation for it altogether. Instead of going back to school, I took on a sales job and focused on making money.

Sales could be exhausting and relentless. This was great for me, since that was my usual pace, but the problem was I felt no satisfaction or fulfillment in my role. I had no group, and I had to feel like I belonged—I needed my tribe.

The work also lacked excitement. There was no action, no uncertainty. Every day was the same. The best I could drum up for any sense of exhilaration was hosting happy hour with a bunch of older lady accountants and letting them grope the shit out of me like a Hooters waitress, all in hopes that they would have their clients use the payroll product I was selling.

I was fortunate to run into my roommate from Ft. Lewis one day and we began swapping stories of what we had been up to in the last year. He was an officer in Kansas City and his patrol stories made me jealous—he promised it was not like being a cop in the Army. It was then that I knew I had to make a change in order to be happy with my career.

CHAPTER 2
OFFICER CARTWRIGHT

Shit, I gotta take a piss.

I groaned, shifting uncomfortably as I stood beside two police officers, towering over a dead woman's bloody body on a dingy apartment floor. A crescent-shaped red stain pooled around her head like a halo. Her brain bubbled out of the hole in her forehead and onto the carpet—it looked like cauliflower blooming from her skull as the pressure from the blood behind the wound increased.

"Shouldn'ta drank that 44, buddy," Officer Turner said, laughing, without taking his eyes off the clipboard in his hand.

"Where's the boyfriend?" Turner asked his partner, who was posted in the front doorway of the apartment.

"Cuffed in the wagon. Just keeps crying and saying they were arguing, and he was trying to take his gun apart and accidentally shot her in the head."

I looked back down at the woman—her head blown open

over everything, right in front of her kids, the contents of her head smattered across the kitchen wall—as officers cordoned off the crime scene.

"I've gotta get the fuck out of here and try to find a bathroom," I said, with more than a quarter of a gallon of Mountain Dew welling in my bladder. I pushed past the crime scene and out beneath the awning of the apartment building, eyeing the prisoner transport van with the woman's boyfriend in the backseat, his face puffed up and streaked with tears.

Rot in hell, fucking asshole!

I hated guys like him—wife beaters who'd turn on the waterworks only after their tempers had gotten the best of them. I scanned the parking lot for the closest bathroom—nothing. Then my eyes gravitated toward a thicket of woods near the edge of the property.

I'm a dude. I'll pee outside, no big deal, I thought.

By this time, the media had shown up. Silver flashes of light from press cameras streaked the black asphalt as news channels filmed in the distance. With everyone distracted, I had no problem sneaking over to the bushes and unzipping my pants. Mid-leak, I heard a rustling behind me.

"HEY!" a man's voice bellowed. "WHO THE FUCK ARE YOU?" Two other voices murmured lower than the man's voice as a stream of light peeked over my shoulder, illuminating the brush in front of me.

"Just a second!" I exclaimed, hurriedly zipping up my fly. Instinctively, I threw both hands in the air and bellowed, "I'm Cartwright, I'm doing a pre-employment ride along. I'm with Officer Turner, and I had to piss, man . . ."

Now zipped up, I swiveled around and squinted into the blinding beam of a flashlight. Three men stood wearing slacks, dress shirts, and loose ties. I knew who they were before they even told me: homicide detectives.

"Get the fuck out of these woods. You're pissing in my crime scene."

"A crime scene? Over here?" I asked, noticing officers taping off the parameters of the woods.

"Yeah, the woman who was killed had kicked her boyfriend out of the apartment weeks ago—he'd been squatting in these bushes, stalking her every move before he finally put a bullet in her head," the detective stated.

"Well, fuck me," I chuckled nervously. "I'll get out of your way." I shuffled past the detectives to go find Turner. As I watched the media swarm and the flurry of activity of medics and coroners arriving at the scene, I felt something exciting—a stirring.

Once we'd climbed back into the cab of the police car, I reached for my still-icy 44 oz cup and took a sip of the half-inch of watered-down soda that was left. I called my Army buddy to tell him how the night was going.

"Sounds like a fun night. You know you need to do this job, right?"

"I know it—" I replied, excited and a little nervous about how I was going to convince Wesley to let me take it, considering the pay cut and type of work. "I'm in."

I graduated from the Kansas City Police Academy in 2007 after an eight-month-long, ass-whooping application process full of standardized tests, psych evals, and having my brain raked over while hooked to a polygraph test, followed by six months in the academy.

Just like in military training, I realized the lessons learned in the police academy could be summated in principles. During my first two nights on the job, I would learn about the importance of command presence, not only in dire situations but among my fellow officers, by whom I was rejected from the start.

"I'm Cartwright, what's up?" I said, waving to the crusty-ass veterans at the inner-city station I'd been assigned to on my first night of patrol. Zero response. I was already nervous and excited by the unknown that awaited me as I adjusted the forty-pound vest and gear that weighed me down in the ruthless August heat. The veterans' faces were deadpan, identical to the response I'd gotten from the old timers in my first unit in the Army.

Guess I'm not making any fucking friends here, I gathered pretty quickly. Once again, I'd been put with the types of guys who were unhappy with their current lives, including their spouses; meanwhile, I was set to marry Wesley in just a few months and, at twenty-eight, I was the happiest I'd ever been now that I wasn't in the sales industry. During mandatory icebreakers and introductions, I shared details of my upcoming wedding with the group, and it only seemed to reinvigorate the vets' disdain for me. They openly planned meetups during our shift and on days off, making it a point to let me know I was not invited. So, I shut the fuck up like a good new guy and waited for my field training officer, who would be responsible for directing me through the next eight weeks of training.

Kurtis Anderson was the name of my FTO—he was quick to pull me aside after roll call to give me some advice.

"Look, dude, I'm gonna shoot straight with you. We are all freshly divorced, so nobody wants to hear about your stupid wedding. Just keep your mouth shut and understand that you don't know shit."

I opened my mouth, ready to launch into a defense, but he continued, "You're not going to answer any—and I mean any—calls on your first night. We're just going to drive around the city so you can get a sense of the layout—no maps, just you, navigating the streets."

I understood this to be the expectation of the KCPD from training; I'd already studied the blueprint of a city that rivaled NYC in size.

"We'll visit all the area hospitals first," he continued, "because if your partner's ever shot or hurt, you're gonna need to be able to locate the closest emergency room immediately. Got it?"

The pressure to do everything as perfectly as possible was real because KCPD axed new officers in a heartbeat. Though graduates were given a "break-in" period while training for the job, if an officer couldn't figure out how to work all the equipment, conduct calls safely, or figure out the geography of the city, they'd be done. I had a good sense of direction, but I hadn't driven around the city that much; as we took to the streets, I learned that they were laid out in a grid system. The best way, I found, was to memorize every street in every direction by heart and repeat, repeat, repeat until I felt sick to my stomach.

Anderson and I spent the next eight hours patrolling the city together. He was deliberate in his instruction, waterboarding me with information, which would be to my benefit (though it didn't feel like it at the time). When our shift ended at 6 a.m., he gave me a rundown of what to expect the following night, when I would be left to accomplish everything that we'd just gone through together on my own.

In an effort for me to learn to do the job, I would be left to make ALL decisions by myself. Anderson would only be there to grade me and do performance reviews afterward (and, on really important calls, to gently prod me toward the correct course of action). My backup was only there in case the situation got out of hand, not to feed me all the answers—otherwise, I wouldn't learn all the hard lessons. In Kansas City, we were so busy and shorthanded that we handled a lot of calls alone, except for the most violent ones. So, I could not do my job if I didn't learn how to do it solo.

"You'll have an officer to assist you on calls, but we're really throwing you into the fire on this one, Cartwright. You'll patrol the city on your own, and you'll be able to recognize pretty quickly if you've got what it takes to stay on."

The following morning at 1:12 a.m., I would receive a call that confirmed every fucking word that my FTO had promised.

I squinted at street signs as Anderson and I did a loop around the city, practicing one more run to the hospital on the outskirts of town. That's when the radio crackled to life announcing a rape call at 1700 Independence Avenue and my sergeant's voice came over the radio, "Good recruit call."

I looked at Anderson who gave me a nod as I answered up to take this call.

My stomach flipped as I tried to figure out where I was going with no map—I quickly realized it was near the 7-Eleven on Independence Avenue, a street where prostitutes would turn tricks for cigarettes and just a few dollars. Many of them struggled with addiction and would have done *anything* for a hookup. I was about to be thrown into the deep end, and I was sure that I was ready to swim.

I rolled up in front of the location to the sound of a woman screaming. When I approached her and introduced myself, she cried hysterically. I invited her to take a seat on the curb, then took to questioning the shit out of her.

"Ma'am, are you okay?" *Umm, no dumbass, of course she isn't.* "Can you tell me what happened?" I asked, standing over her with my notepad and pen in hand.

"Well, we were just drinking and smoking. Then, that motherfucker raped me." As she continued her story, I focused on her every word. *I'm not missing a fucking thing,* I promised myself. I got as many details on the page as possible: his appearance, the make of his car, anything that would help us find him. While we spoke, my sergeant, Deb, pulled up, wanting to check in with the woman on how I was handling things.

"Let me in here, Cartwright," she said. Clearly unhappy

with me, she continued, "Go over there and talk to your assisting officer." I followed orders. I walked over to my assisting officer's car and showed him my notes.

"So, what are you going to do?" he asked.

"Truthfully? I don't have a fucking clue," I said, gesturing toward the woman who was still with Deb.

"All right . . . see how upset she still is, Cartwright? Any idea why that could be?"

I stared at him with a stupid look on my face.

"Well, do you think a woman who was just traumatized by a man really wants to be grilled with questions from a guy who's twice her size and is towering over her?"

"I—I didn't think of that," I stammered as my backup pointed back to Deb, who'd sat down with the woman on the curb and was talking to her at eye level.

"Rule number one: don't fucking re-traumatize a rape victim, idiot," he stated. I nodded, indicating I understood, clutching my notebook hard, unable to get a full breath. My backup continued prepping me to ask the woman questions when she leaped to her feet and began shrieking.

"THERE HE GOES! THERE THAT MOTHERFUCKER GOES. RIGHT THERE!" She extended her bony arm, pointing at a rickety blue Toyota Corolla speeding past.

"THAT MOTHERFUCKER OWES ME $20. I WANT MY $20. If he doesn't pay me, I want to press fucking charges! I'll prosecute his ass!"

Sickness washed over me as she continued to wail, long after the car was out of sight.

Deb stood up from the stoop and approached me.

"Well, Cartwright, what do you got?"

What do I have? What should I do? I have no idea what to do! I warred.

"Let's get the guy pulled over and have someone arrest him, and let's order an ambulance for her," I replied, trying to sound confident.

Eavesdropping, the victim waved wildly from the stoop, "NO! I don't want no ambulance. NO AMBULANCE!" she screamed.

I stepped aside and returned to my car to call one of the detectives who specifically handled sexual assault cases.

"It sounds like this is a situation of non-pay," the detective explained.

"Non-pay?" I asked.

Non-pay is a term for when prostitutes perform sexual acts *before* receiving payment; it was likely the guy kicked her out of his car before paying her. This was unfortunately super common in this area, and I would learn that a prosecutor would never take that seriously. The best bet was to send her to the hospital, have her get a SANE exam, find the guy and get all the information out of him we could, if we could stop him from fleeing.

I walked back to the victim and gave her a few options but let her know that we couldn't arrest this guy for rape. She refused any further assistance and walked off screaming, "FUCK YOU! FUCKING WORTHLESS FUCKING PIGS!" I was quickly learning that this was a completely different world than I had realized.

I ended the call with my emotions bottomed out. I'd gone from the paralyzing fear of reporting a rape, to getting my dick kicked in by my backup for towering over the poor woman in a power stance, to realizing the lady just wanted to retaliate and had no interest in really getting any help at all.

"Fuck, man! You're driving through a goddamn crime scene!" Anderson yelled as I pulled up near the pavilion in the center of a poorly lit city park.

"What the fuck? Man, you told me I parked too far away!" I blared, hands trembling on the steering wheel.

"Yeah, well, I didn't tell you to park on top of the guy, Jesus Christ! Back up off 'im." I put the car in reverse, then slammed it into park. My body rocked as I looked up to Anderson, as if he were about to tell me what to do.

"We need more cars over here at 27th and Garfield," warbled a voice over the radio. It was my first shooting, so I'd rushed to the scene, unsure of what I'd roll into. One man was down; he lay in front of my car, body limp like a ragdoll. A group of screaming, crying folks stood around him.

I thrust open the car door and the tinny smell of blood hit my nose. Anderson ambled beside me as I rounded the front of my vehicle, car lights shining on the broken, lifeless body sprawled out on the drought-plagued grass, shadows of the sixty-acre park in the distance enveloped in night. The surrounding neighborhood was a blighted area. Half of the houses were boarded up; the park was known to be a place overrun by gang members and dope slingers. A backup officer kept his distance from the grisly crowd as an ambulance wailed in the distance, waiting for me to determine the crime scene "clear" so they could examine the body.

"HELP! HE'S SHOT!" yelled an emaciated woman with gaps in her teeth, wearing an oversized jersey, star leggings, and flip flops. Tears streamed down her face. She appeared to know the guy.

"HE'S DYING! DO SOMETHING, MOTHERFUCKERS!" called a kid, no older than fifteen, wearing sagging pants, black basketball shoes, and an oversized white T-shirt.

I hadn't seen a lot of dead people yet, but even I knew the dude was dead—like fucking dead-dead. *What the fuck do they want me to do?*

The man laid face-down on his stomach. Anderson extended his gloved hand, calmly waving a black latex clump in my direction. I grabbed the gloves from him, slid them over my hands, then turned the man over as his fractured skull began to leak mangled mush and part of an eyeball. He looked like a pumpkin that had been carved, then left outside in the sun for too long.

"What the fuck are you waiting for? DO FUCKIN' SOMETHING!" the gaunt woman continued to yell.

I checked for his heartbeat and there was, of course, no pulse, then carried out a few rounds of CPR, to no avail.

"Get the ambulance in here—" I said to Anderson, still kneeling beside the man's head. Anderson bent his head down and spoke into the corded receiver attached to his right shoulder.

"Cartwright—" Anderson said, squatting as he spoke, "Maybe those people are witnesses?" He nodded to the group, cluing me in to my next step.

I stood up, composed myself, and walked toward the group.

"Okay, y'all," I addressed them, reaching for the pen and tiny notepad I'd tucked into my shirt pocket like they did on TV. "Did anyone see what happened?"

There were varied reactions among the group: brows furrowed with irritation, arms crossed, bodies backed away. A couple of guys even peeled away from the group, stepping far back.

"Can I get some of your names?" I pressed, inciting an uproar.

"Whoa, whoa, whoa—why do you need our names?" one of the group members asked.

"Nah! We ain't givin' you our names. We ain't seen shit!" yelled the kid in the white shirt.

"Go fuck yourself! We don't even know that guy!" one woman called out, pointing at the kid on the ground.

"He probably got what he fucking deserved!" someone called from the back.

Several began to leave the scene, which caused me to panic.

Shit! What the fuck do I do now? They're leaving a crime scene! How many of them could we even catch and handcuff?

One woman chose to cooperate; the rest gave her looks like she'd regret it as they sunk back into the shadows to watch the incident play out.

I wrote down every detail I could (though all were pretty unhelpful). In truth, I wasn't prepared for the disdain I received just for the uniform I wore. Day after day, the people I encountered absolutely hated me, all because of my blue shirt and badge. This was in stark contrast to all the meals random strangers had paid for when they overheard that I was in the Army. Here, I was seen as the enemy, even when that same person had called 911 on their drunk spouse.

Our society fails to realize that police work is a dirty business. It's easy to look at it from the sanctity of the suburbs or low-crime areas and pass judgment on all cops when some dumbass cop makes the national news. But the truth is, on this earth, there are bad people in every profession—see priests and teachers having sex with kids or famous actors being outed for sexual assault. I hated to admit it, but I was guilty of the same judgment—that police are all assholes—until I put myself in their boots.

As I looked at the woman who stared back at me with wide eyes, I steadied myself. I asked her things like her last name, address, and social security number—she'd conveniently "forgot" all three, and I realized the group as a whole would be uncooperative. I pleaded with several of them, causing them to wave me off or laugh in my face before abandoning the scene.

Anderson sensed my frustration and knew it was time to level with me. "Dude, you can't pussyfoot around with these people. You gotta take control, man. Only new guys are out here begging people to cooperate. You've gotta act like you been on for a decade. Dude's fucking dead. Your only hope is that some of these people will talk to the detectives, but they can't talk to them if you let them leave without identifying them."

Like always, Anderson was right.

Since the radio had called for more cars, the park was flooded with old timers; for better or worse, they had an entirely different, "fuck all" approach. To them, this guy was just another corpse to be scraped off the ground. They joked and shot the shit on the perimeter of the crime scene, conscious enough of what they were doing to turn their backs to the media once they'd turned up with microphones and the cameras were rolling. A man had just been executed and they were over there, scratching their balls, probably making dirty jokes about the "sweet young thing" reporting for Channel Five News. I swore to myself that I'd *never* become that cold. Meanwhile, the group of witnesses who wouldn't trust me with details were now unloading on the homicide detectives who had emerged on the scene. They didn't trust me, and I couldn't blame them—I couldn't trust myself, Officer Cartwright, either.

What was worse was how I felt returning to my quiet home, just after sunrise. I creaked open the front door to find Wesley curled up on the couch in her fuzzy robe, looking well-rested with a steaming cup of coffee in hand while I smelled like nighttime, salty sweat, and patrol car. I kissed her cheek.

"How was last night, babe?" she asked, as I collapsed into the cushion beside her, covering my head and rubbing my temples.

"Well," I said, "a guy had his brains blown out in the park. It was pretty bad. There were brains all over the crime scene, which I fucking parked in and almost drove over. Since I was on the scene, Anderson and I had to stay there for hours because the car had to be taped off."

Her gentle hand rubbed the tense muscles in my back as she continued to ask questions.

"Oh my God, that's so scary. How did you handle that?"

she asked. Wesley was a teacher, and a great one. She was, and still is, the sweetest person alive—she's very emotional, and one of the best communicators I've ever met. She knew that if this had happened to *her*, she would need to talk it out for hours to free herself from what she had just witnessed. I didn't pick up on it then, but it was almost as if she was trying to impart some wisdom early on to deal with the hell I would be facing throughout my career.

It was a good question; one I actually had to sit and think about.

"I don't know, babe, I was just pissed," I said.

"Pissed?" she questioned. "That's . . . interesting. Why do you say that?"

I drew a breath and thought for a moment. In these early months of working on patrol, I would come home and tell Wesley everything, all the details and the crazy stories and my feelings about what I had experienced. She, just like all my non-cop buddies, were drawn to the hell that society can be in the worst parts of our city. It's no wonder there are so many cop shows—people are just drawn to it like a car wreck. They crane their necks to see and I happily obliged whenever asked, sparing no details whatsoever. Wesley wasn't into these stories out of morbid curiosity. She genuinely appreciated the work I did and the sacrifices I made for my country and my community. It was me who couldn't help but to overindulge in the details as she attentively soaked in my satisfaction with my new career.

"Well," I began, "the random assholes who knew what happened were acting so goddamn stupid that I could hardly focus on the dead guy lying on the ground. I literally stepped out of the car and the smell hit my nose. Fresh blood. The blood of someone's son—maybe someone's brother or father. But I was so inundated with bullshit, I could hardly feel anything at all, and I just think—I just had to act. This is how people get really, really fucked up in this job."

Wesley's body pressed into my shoulder as she leaned into me. She rested her hand on my cheek, prompting me to turn my head until we were eye-to-eye.

"Brent, *you're* gonna be okay doing this job, right? Promise me you won't lose sight of what's important. Promise me this job won't change you," she pressed.

"I got this, babe." I sighed, desperate for it to be possible; desperate to cling to my humanity for as long as I could.

Within my first six months of being in the department, I'd seen nothing but gory crime scenes, and all while trying to tolerate the apathy of the citizens I was sworn to protect. I lived in a swell of adrenaline, anticipating the endless stupidity that people call 911 for, but when I'd show up on the scene, a wall would go up between me and everyone I interacted with, no matter how grotesque the situation. I wrestled with whether my ability to compartmentalize was serving me. On one hand, it helped me understand who I wanted to be as a cop and how I could help people as Officer Cartwright. On the other hand, I started to become jaded toward all of society, even when I was off the clock. I would see a victim or someone who had a negative experience and start blaming them for it. It was as though I was beginning to live two lives. I'd disregard the overall disconnect I had between myself and the world, because there were certain parts of the job that were really fun, like car chases, foot chases, and nightly fights with criminals who gave zero fucks that I was a police officer.

Being a cop taught me I had so many sides to myself: the Real Brent Cartwright (who needed to feel in control, loved serving his community, and sought the invigorating adrenaline the job fed him), Officer Cartwright (who clung to his values, knowing why he wanted to chase bad guys, and enjoyed being in uniform and part of a tribe), and Hotshot Brent Cartwright (a go-getter who stopped people right and left, who loved taking control in a hectic scene, who got high from foot-chasing bad guys and wrestling them into handcuffs). I thought all of those Brents were pretty fucking cool.

Then, in 2008, all three Brent Cartwrights were humbled. While conducting surveillance on a dope complaint, I watched as a car thief broke into a dark-blue Ford Explorer and tried to steal it. I got cocky with the thief I snuck up on, pulling him out of the car window before he knew what hit him. The fight was on and got out of hand when the guy hopped up from the ground and swung at me with a screwdriver in his hand, narrowly avoiding burying it deep in my neck. I reacted without thinking and lunged at him, slamming him to the ground in the pile of broken glass and pinning that motherfucker with all my weight. This was a serious fight, a fight for my own life as I focused on taking the weapon while simultaneously absorbing several punches to my own face with his other hand.

I was forced to (violently) disarm him in this all-out street brawl. I brought a slightly higher level of aggression, unknowingly pressing his face into a pile of broken glass shards that we were fighting in. I didn't know it then, but the glass became lodged into his eyeball during our fight. As I countered his punches with my own, I drove the glass deeper and deeper into his eye until he finally tired and quit punching. I got him in handcuffs and found he was here illegally from Guatemala, willing to do anything to avoid being deported. Even if it meant killing a cop. Motherfucker went to jail, lost an eye, then slapped me with an excessive force complaint even as he admitted to trying to stab me.

I would get two more notices of excessive force complaints that same week, which were also bullshit. Suddenly, I was painted as the "cop who beats the shit out of people" by the Major in charge of our division, and I was under investigation by internal affairs for *all three* incidents. Deb took up residency in my asshole and made it clear that it was in my best interest to slow down my work pace until the investigations were completed. Veteran officers would comfort me, letting me know this was just part of the job and that officers willing to bust their ass and work hard would inevitably get bullshit complaints at a higher rate than others. With a target on my back, I really thought things couldn't get worse, then of-fucking-course they did.

In December, I responded to an injury car accident on the interstate that left me pinned between a stupid drunk girl's bumper and the pavement as she raced toward the shoulder of the blocked roadway. She'd been defiant and refused to get out of the car. The usual method would have been to open the door and get her out of her car, even if she fought back.

However, I reached through the open window, took her keys, and waited for backup just as I had been advised. It just so happened she had another set of keys on hand and started her car, then began fleeing the scene. She rolled me over, sending me skidding across four lanes of highway, and I slammed head-first into a guardrail. She left my body crumpled, covered in scrapes and gashes, and then she sped off. As traumatic as it was, all I could do was be physically evaluated, then get back to the grind. I suffered in pain for a few months before I finally got an MRI and found that my shoulder was shredded and would require surgery.

Following surgery, I was placed on limited duty, which meant a day shift for the first time in years. Living on a regular daytime schedule, I was actually able to be present at home, which meant that it only took a few months for Wesley to become pregnant. Several months later, I finally healed enough and came right back to my tribe—my squad of veterans where I now belonged.

My time with the team was short-lived, as Wesley and I welcomed our first daughter, Brenley, in early 2010. I made it a point to be attentive—to really be there. I went to every doctor's appointment and took the full twelve weeks of paternity leave by using my sick leave. During that time, Wesley and I traveled to visit her mother and relatives in Pennsylvania and Chicago, followed by visits to my family in Oklahoma to show off our amazing gift. This was an awesome time, and I never even thought about work. I diverted work calls as I gladly made my family my priority. I jumped at the chance to change every diaper and take on any wakeup duty I could so Wesley could rest.

When I came back from my leave, life was back to normal, and I was out chasing bad guys as if I'd never left. My motivation, along with that of my great friend, Roger, seemed to bring our entire squad into a much happier place. Like a puppy with an old dog, there was a new spark in all of us.

With this newly invigorated group in full action, positive things started to happen. Piece by piece, my squad left for greener pastures and transferred to different specialized units within our department. Considering that I wasn't a newbie anymore, though still the low man on the totem pole, I stood by and waited for my turn. Unfortunately, with the economy in the crapper, a hiring and pay freeze took hold, so my wait became longer than I anticipated.

In the blink of an eye, I found myself in year five of my career, being paid like I was in year two, surrounded by a kinder, gentler (and younger) generation of cops. Don't get me wrong, it wasn't the worst thing in the world to have more empathetic police officers working beats. However, the harshness of society in our inner city tended to capitalize on timid and seemingly weak cops. I had zero tolerance for losing to bad guys, but this new breed of cop was letting it happen nightly.

I know that my drive is much higher than that of most folks. I always strive to be the best. But I chose a humble approach, carrying and teaching those performing at a lesser standard rather than ridiculing and leaving them behind. But even that was a challenge as burnout set in. I eventually became the same disgruntled and grumpy cop I encountered on my first day at roll call, fresh out of the academy. The only way I could lift myself out of this burnout and depression was to make a change. This pivot became clear to me when I, yet again, found myself talking to a friend I hadn't seen in a few years.

A good buddy of mine who was working undercover called me and asked if I wanted to get a drink and catch up. He was a classmate of mine from the academy—a guy I highly respected. I met him for drinks and listened to his stories like some groupie. He talked about drug busts and living life on a steady diet of caffeine and adrenaline, then he expressed his desire to come back to patrol and put undercover work behind him.

"I just don't get it, man," I pressed. "How could you leave a job where you get to do so much cool shit?"

He shook his head at my question, then gruffly responded, "Easily, dude. It starts to get to you after a while and I miss being a cop. Most people only last a year and a half in that job, if that. All of us start out excited, but we get beaten down pretty quickly. This job can eat you alive."

Despite his warning, I was immediately sold—*this* was what I wanted to do. It was just what I needed to pull me out of my slump and I would stop at nothing to get it. My one problem was figuring out how I'd sell Wesley on this new gig.

Days later, I pitched the idea to my wife knowing I would do ANYTHING to get her to agree to it. I started with the positives: it was mostly day shifts, and I'd have weekends off. Fortunately, I'd kept true to myself and had been open and honest with her over every close call that nearly took my life. I went for the emotional touch and reminded her that I had been run over by two different cars and had faced countless fights with armed people trying to kill me. All things that wouldn't happen as an undercover—*or so I'd have her believe.*

Then, I told her a washed down version of the work and sold her on how safe it was. To drive my point home, I even invited my friend and his wife over to answer some of her questions. With a cleaned-up version of what I would really be doing settling into her mind, she was convinced that this transfer was good and gave me the nod. Then, I braced myself for another grueling round of being the new guy. I welcomed the prospect of establishing yet *another* identity in my ever-shifting career. I was already primed for this job as far as my young family was concerned. My time in uniform with a small baby at home had conditioned me to compartmentalize my loved ones in my mind, allowing me to face these violent streets daily without distraction.

CHAPTER 3
THE BIRTH OF RICKY

After getting my transfer approved for the undercover squad, I left my work as a patrol officer in the rearview mirror forever. Overnight, I found a renewed excitement for my career. I'd always been a highly motivated, goal-driven person, and now I was ready to prove myself to my new squad. Gone were the days of dreading going to work in my blues around familiar grumps. I made myself a promise to never again dedicate my life to work that didn't bring me happiness.

This transfer would also usher my undercover identity, Richard Vaughn Kimball, into the world: "Ricky" for short. I'd been the one tasked with creating a name and identity. Once I'd developed a personality, I'd be taken down to the state capitol to receive a new driver's license to make Ricky official.

When asked why I'd chosen the name Ricky, I explained that I liked Rick Vaughn, Charlie Sheen's character from the

1989 movie *Major League*. Truthfully, I really wanted something easy to remember. I made Vaughn my middle name, so it wasn't so obvious that my identity was fake. I happened to be planted in front of a television while making my choice when Harrison Ford flashed across the screen in the movie *The Fugitive*. His name: Richard Kimball. *A perfect coincidence.* So, my new undercover identity was born.

I showed up for my first day already riding the high of the job, and I hadn't done anything except gas up my undercover car. I'd been told to come to work completely filthy, dressed in the shittiest clothes I could find. Even Wesley found my new "uniform" convincing as she winced at the loss of her crew cut husband. I was assigned to an experienced undercover who would be my FTO, and he'd already informed me that my training would be gradual. My first week mostly consisted of doing surveillance for other officers' undercover deals to get a feel for how the squad worked. The excitement to get to work and prove to everyone that I belonged was overwhelming. I craved the high of a deal, which was crazy to say since I literally had never been close to anything like it in my life.

I spent most of the first morning being escorted through our covert building and going over paperwork. By noon, I was feeling restless. I was ready to get out of the office and do something. My anticipation of working with my new squad was showing (something I'd inevitably be hazed for). The problem was that this group of undercovers had been in this squad for a few years, and they were severely burned out. All had been promised new assignments to more coveted positions where the work was less taxing and more appreciated, but they had yet to be moved. This left me listening to the group as they expressed their wishes to leave, emphasizing only the worst parts of our job.

None of what they were saying made any sense to me.

Don't they know how great they have it? I wondered.

To me, this seemed to be the best job in the world. So, I made it my goal to bring the same energy to this group that I brought to my patrol squad when I first started.

It was common for new undercovers to come into their assignments with stomachs full of nerves and a fear of the unknown. The drug world is the Wild-fucking-West. It's not something anyone could prepare for without *living* it.

I started this work thinking I knew enough from my arrests and patrols. My FTO, Kyle, tried explaining that this was *not* the world I'd known as a uniformed officer. But I sensed he could see the wild hunger in my eyes. He knew I was barely listening to him. Kyle also seemed to recognize that I was different from the previous newbie undercovers. There was not an ounce of reservation in my mind to go out on the streets.

"You need to lose all of your police-isms first," Kyle (and the squad) insisted. They knew the people on the street would see right through the cheap disguise I was wearing and call me on my bullshit.

Hanging back while my squad members were out doing continual drug buys made me feel like a weak link, and I had to learn to accept that I was. I was brand new and still working leads at a fraction of my colleagues' paces. Feeling like "the slug" of the group motivated me to try even harder.

My early work involved going through a list of potential

dealers and making cold calls (not dissimilar to a sales position). I would make so many calls that my cell phone would be dead by noon. To my benefit, the squad gave me a big pat on the back any time I lined up a buy over a cold call. They would drop what they were doing and give me their full attention, making me feel like a contributor to the team.

The files I was given consisted of countless "tips" that had been called in from all over the city. Scorned lovers or dope buyers selling out their dealers, their stash houses, and phone numbers in the name of revenge. I discovered several complaints about two men named Kenny and Jake who were selling meth and engaging in prostitution at an HIV discussion group. Kenny was a man in his upper forties, and Jake was an eighteen-year-old kid being taken advantage of. Our squad focused on dope and guns only, so the sex stuff just got ignored unless it helped the buy.

Having never attended a group meeting for any reason, my only guess was that it was similar to the group meetings in the movie *Fight Club*, but with sex instead of fist fights. The complaint was very specific about how these two men conducted their business. They attended the HIV help group at a small hotel downtown, which was actually a home converted into a gay male-only inn. Following the meetings, Kenny and Jake would allegedly throw meth-fueled parties in the basement, where Jake performed sex acts on anyone who showed interest and had a shockingly small amount of cash.

I had to get into character before I called Kenny. As an undercover, I would have to alter Ricky's recreational drug habits multiple times per day: meth head, heroin shooter, crack addict—they all had different mannerisms and

THE BIRTH OF RICKY

personas unique to their respective drug culture. Within each grouping, I'd find unique subsets. On this day, I would enter the homosexual pocket of the meth world.

I called Kenny and made it clear what I was after: a meth fix. I tried to convince him that he'd instructed me to call him at an HIV meeting for a hookup. Kenny didn't seem put off by this, but he said he didn't remember me. For this reason, he would not commit to meeting me outside the meetings.

On that same phone call, he hung up on me. He screened my call every time I tried to phone him back, but I was persistent. I pressured myself to keep pace with my squad, which led me to start texting Kenny without even thinking.

Whose dick do I have to suck to get the hookup around here? I shot.

That got an immediate response.

Meet me at the gas station at 39th and Broadway in seven minutes.

The deal was on. Or so I thought.

Of course, Kyle was livid, reminding me I was supposed to be buying dope, not trying to get a dick in my mouth. I sat in my undercover car, letting my anticipation build as I prepared for the buy, playing out countless scenarios in my head of how things would go, before finally working up the courage to text Kenny.

I'M HERE. Where are you?

No answer.

After a few minutes, the phone rang. I glanced at the caller ID, hoping to see Kenny's name. Instead, it was Kyle.

"What's the plan, Ricky?" he asked. I begged for more time, telling him that I knew I could get this done.

I waited, restless, for five minutes, seven minutes, ten minutes—when suddenly, a pair who fit the profile of what I was looking for appeared on the street corner: an older man with bleach-blonde spiked hair, a black T-shirt, and ripped up jeans, standing beside a young man wearing sweatpants and a dirty maroon T-shirt. They lingered there for several minutes, scanning the area for the person who had been texting them. I locked eyes with who I assumed to be Kenny, cracked my window, and then gave him a nod.

He nudged the young man in my direction, and within seconds, the two were nearing my car.

As they got closer to the vehicle, I said in my most effeminate voice, "What's up?"

With zero hesitation, Jake opened the car door and slid into the backseat while Kenny walked around to the passenger door, pulled it open, and then took his place beside me.

"Do you recognize him?" Kenny questioned Jake right in front of me.

"Come the fuck on," I pressed. "Stop fucking with me."

Kenny glanced at Jake, who sat quietly in the back seat. I watched his tiny arms shrug in the rearview mirror. We made small talk about where we hung out together and how we had met. I fed them total bullshit and lies the entire time.

"All right—fine, fine," Kenny said. "It's going to take us ten minutes. Give us your money."

"Dude, I don't think so."

I clutched the steering wheel, avoiding eye contact, worried I'd give myself away if I looked at either of them for too long.

"All right, man, just stay put," Kenny conceded. "We're going to go back right now and get it. Just give us a few minutes."

He signaled to Jake, then they both opened their car doors and exited the vehicle at the same time. As they left, I was overcome by a sinking feeling.

This isn't going to happen. Fuck! Fuck! Fuck!

My phone immediately rang. It was Kyle. I explained the situation, to which he responded, "Look, Ricky, if they're not back in five minutes, you get the hell out of there. We're wasting time."

"Got it," I stated, then hung up the phone.

Sure as shit, after five minutes, the two rounded the street corner, headed in my direction.

This time, Jake walked to my window and Kenny stayed at a good distance.

"Okay, so, where's your money?" Jake asked.

"Where's the shit?"

"Right here," he replied, shaking his closed palm in my direction.

"Let me see it," I insisted.

"It's right here," he said, waving his tight fist, still refusing to give me a glimpse of the drugs.

Finally, anxious to make this a success, I pulled out my money, and he reached through the window quickly, trying to snatch the wad of cash out of my hand. In the swirling motion of it all, I caught a glimpse of what he was actually holding: a tiny plastic bag of weed. *Weed!* Only weed. Twenty dollars' worth of weed at most. Weed was still illegal at the time, but nobody gave a shit about it. This motherfucker was trying to rip me off.

Fuck it, I thought, *I came all the way here. I'm gonna buy something ... anything ...*

I made the exchange, and then Jake walked away from my car. The two began to walk back towards the street corner.

"Hey, I'll be in touch!" I called after them. I finally left the gas station, my tiny bag of weed in hand, which would send Kyle through the roof. As my deals with Kenny progressed, I had to continually fight off him and Jake trying to rope me into threesomes—or, at a minimum, trying to jack me off within a minute of walking into their apartment. This assignment was full of things I never expected from police work. When I got home, I would tell Wesley everything and joke that, no matter how dirty I appeared, I was irresistible to everyone.

My first "official" attempt at a cold drug buy on the street happened near a rundown laundromat on Bales Avenue, just off Ninth Street, two days after I started in the undercover squad. Kyle had driven me to the area to scope out a party scene that regularly took place in the vacant lot beside the establishment. Everything on that side of town had basically gone to shit; neither Kyle nor I could confirm whether the business was actually operating as there were no cars in the parking lot in the middle of the day.

Kyle took me to this part of town because it was flooded with users and dealers of crack cocaine. Of course, we had to drive in *his* car. He'd been on a special assignment, so it was sparkling clean, unlike mine, which smelled like rotted hell. He wanted nothing to do with riding in it. Once we'd cut through the laundromat parking lot, where we saw what we'd expected to see: a crowd of fifteen or so black men and women standing around, drinking, smoking cigarettes, and being loud as fuck at four in the afternoon. The sun had by no means set, but the sky was slush-water gray and had turned eerie. The scene was one I'd encountered many times on patrol—groups in the fucking hood partying all day and into the early morning.

Kyle idled for an uncomfortably long time, facing the small patch of earth along the side of the building where the group was gathered. In the spring, the space was covered in patches of green, but in the winter, it became packed mud that was slick to the touch. I couldn't imagine why anyone would choose this as a place to hang out. I pondered this as Kyle intermittently crept the car closer, not considering how awkward it would be to have the whole group turn and stare at us in his fancy, black Toyota. Through the windshield, I could see the group stiffening.

Kyle may have been a good undercover cop, but he was a moron when it came to social cues, and he had seemingly lost his street smarts. A very important rule of the streets: don't point at people. It's a major sign of disrespect, and it will *always* create issues. And in Kansas City, it can bring bullets your way. Naturally, he started assessing the situation, verbalizing his thoughts to me, and moving his index finger around like a lunatic.

"You should just walk right up to 'em—right in the middle there," he said, extending his arm.

"Dude! Do you have to point at them? Even I know better than that!" I exclaimed. "Could you at least drop me around the corner or something, so I don't have to be seen with you?"

Kyle sat there for a moment, lost entirely to the left hemisphere of his brain, then posited, "What, are you nervous? Fucking Whitey, you can't be scared to do this job."

I slapped my knee in exasperation, attempting not to make any large gestures from the waist up so as not to be noticed even more by the crowd.

"Dude, of course I'm nervous. Look over there. Look anywhere! Not a single person in five square blocks from here is white, except us, and you're out here pointing at everyone while we're trying to buy dope!"

"Well, there is no 'we're.' It's all you." He laughed. "Problem is, you're a cop and you show it. You walk like a cop, talk like a cop, think like a cop. This isn't about buying dope. Get out there and just talk; learn how to stop acting like a cop." With this, he reached across my lap, opened my door, and nudged me out of the vehicle.

He wasn't exactly wrong about me still reeking of cop. There is a *way* about cops—it's an assuredness we build through training and carry with us, even when we're off duty. It's really hard to let go once we're no longer serving in the same way. I realized almost instantly, as I approached the group, that I looked just as stupid as Kyle to these people.

"What's this white motherfucker doin'?" I heard one of the guys mutter under his breath, causing a group posted up along the wall to break out into raucous laughter.

I felt I was set up for failure by being dropped here. Surely there hadn't been a white guy in the history of dope buying who had walked up to this group and assimilated enough to get a buy. There are very real racial boundaries in this world, even among the addicts and greedy dopers. These rules are to be followed unless you want to get jumped and robbed. A loner who didn't fit in, like me, would be an easy target, and I could only imagine the witnesses having the same amnesia as those I encountered on patrol while working so many homicides. This first attempt reminded me of my basic training tasks—designed with guaranteed failure built into them—but I would be wrong. Later that same year, I would come right back here and do several buys with almost no issue. However, on this particular day, I still had too much of the cop in me and not enough skill for this to be successful.

"I just, uh—What's up?" I asked.

Goddammit. I've already blown it.

"Y'all just . . . hanging out?" I asked, eyeing the place like I'd never seen it before. Several of the girls' expressions twisted like I was the most repulsive loser in the world. Most of the guys were looking around—clearly trying to find the police take-down van—confident I was a cop.

They slowly began to disband, going in all directions: some went further into the back alley behind the building, some toward the front lot that was attached to a sidewalk, some even chose to walk up to Kyle, mere feet away from his car, while staring into his windows and making cop jokes.

"Wait, wait," I said. "Who's got the hookup?"

This caused the group to hasten in every direction until all but three were completely out of sight. The three consisted of two guys and one woman. They remained next to me, puffing on cigarettes and sipping on malt liquor.

"What's up with your boy there?" one of the guys asked, taking a swig from the wrapped forty in his hand, gesturing at Kyle.

I feel it's important to say this about this job: there are times I had to act and say things completely against who I really am. It is a part of working in these streets, I had to adjust how I talked and use words I otherwise would not. "Man, I tell you, he's fucking something—" I said. "Dude's a fag wanting me to suck him off. He gave me his money and wanted me to get some shit. I'm just out here trying to get high; I'm going to fucking run when I get some shit. Who want in?"

I watched their faces contort in painful disbelief as I said this—they winced at my lie; I tried not to break character, but internally, I was wincing too.

"Well, ain't nobody here gonna help you," the guy stated.

"Yeah, we don't mess with that shit, Officer," the girl said, shaking her head.

At that very moment, a big white van whipped into the parking lot, causing the remaining three people to bolt. I knew it was likely that Kyle had called for someone to come get me, as I was fucking this all up and practically begging people to no avail.

The front window rolled down, and a woman's voice called my name from across the parking lot.

"Ricky! Where the fuck you been? Get in!" *Kelly*.

I dashed over, pulled the door on the driver's side open, and clambered into the vehicle.

We sped off, talking only once we'd hit a light one block over.

"How'd it go?" Kelly inquired.

"Yeah, that pretty much sucked. Kyle did me zero favors parking like that."

"Sometimes, I think he just likes to fuck with people. It was bound to happen—we don't get many cold buys over here. None of that group was probably holding anyway. They would've had to call it up regardless. How'd you do talking to people, though?" she questioned.

"Not fucking good," I admitted. "As in, really fucking bad. It is easier said than done."

"How 'bout a few tips," she offered. This was the one thing I grew to appreciate in my short time around Kelly; sure, she always gave me shit in the office, but she was quick to hold the line if any of us ever really needed help. She went on to tell me that I needed a conversation starter.

"The almighty cigarette is king of all social interactions," she said. With that, she handed me a half pack of Pall Malls and kept feeding me tips. "Keep these with you and go get a beer when you try to buy out here cold. When you pull out cigarettes, offer some up, then strike up a conversation and keep it super casual. Remind yourself that you're always in control and quit acting nervous. No one expects you to get a buy. Go fuck with them and have fun."

"Always in control, fuck 'em, have fun—that I can do," I responded. "Thanks."

At that exact moment, Kyle paged us over the radio: "I think I've found another place where Ricky can try, up here on the Avenue. Drop him off with me; I'll get him going."

"Sounds like more practice. It wouldn't hurt to do something crazy," Kelly said, making a hairpin turn that set us off in the opposite direction.

It was almost like she was daring me. And it was just the push I needed.

Prior to being in this squad, I only knew of one incident where an undercover had a gun pulled on them during a deal. The dealer and his friends wanted him to prove he wasn't a cop, so they locked him in a basement using knives to wedge the door closed. Once in the basement, the group pulled a gun on him and attempted to force him to smoke PCP. The SWAT team came in and rescued the officer before anything happened. This situation ended up motivating the detective to transfer back to patrol. Within six months of his extraction, he quit police work altogether.

After I became an undercover, that buy-gone-wrong was the one key teaching point drilled into us during training with our SWAT team. I was assured that being held at gunpoint was rare; in fact, no similar incident had occurred in the two years since the detective had left the squad. This gave me a false sense of security on the job. It was hard to imagine the possibility of being killed over a twenty-dollar crack rock.

My misconception was that big dope deals would be the most dangerous, and my job was not to go after pounds. In reality, the smaller deals were the most volatile. The small dope game is ruled by desperate dealers, so robbing or killing someone over forty dollars was more common than I knew. Weighing the risk versus reward of the job would have prompted any sane person to say "no, thank you" to the position. But I, Ricky Vaughn Kimball, was fucking insane.

In my first month, most of the few buys I could get went smoothly. All in all, I was a pretty agreeable drug addict. I wouldn't argue too much when I'd get shorted on my crack. I knew I'd inevitably be the target of "white boy pricing"—because I was white and buying drugs in parts of town where I was in the minority, I'd never get my money's worth. But, at that point in my career, I didn't care. It wasn't my money, so there was no reason to take it personally. I became a little *too* comfortable with doing buys without conflict. I let my guard down—which is when you can really get burned.

With some of our squad off on vacation, Kyle and I worked shorthanded during my fifth week. I agreed to cover him on his deals, trying hard to hear his verbal exchanges over our crappy listening devices. Then, he would do the same for me.

One Monday, I set up a small marijuana buy from a dealer that I had already used a few times named D, a moniker used by about a million dope dealers. I was so comfortable with this man that I became complacent to his every red flag.

No one fucking cares about marijuana. I was sure. My

previous buys with him were for small amounts—never more than eighty dollars.

When I called D, he was reliable and ready to sell to me, as expected. My previous buys with him had been in a gas station parking lot known as a hotspot for drug deals. It was common for there to be a lot of traffic circling in and out of that area, which was located on a street that required such heavy policing that the lot remained "hidden in plain sight," as officers rarely had time to stop and patrol it. With so many eyes and great high-definition security cameras, dealers and buyers alike felt a strange sense of security. It was a place where almost no one ever got robbed or shot.

However, D demanded that this buy go down differently. He had me head over to an obscure and out-of-the-way gas station on the east side of Kansas City. It was so far off the beaten path that I didn't even know it existed. I had to ask Kyle where the hell it was. This was one of the little missed clues.

When I pulled into the lot, I scanned the area for D's usual banged up Toyota Corolla. Noticing that it wasn't there, I assumed he hadn't arrived yet. I got out of my car and headed in the direction of some bushes, intending to take a piss. I relied upon this move to throw anyone off who might be watching—anyone who might think, *I don't trust this white dude.* As soon as I had my dick in my hand, I was startled by the honk of a blue Chevy Cobalt backed in against the side of the gas station. I glanced up to see D in the driver's seat, nodding for me to walk over to him. I could see the car was loaded up with three other people in it.

I tucked my junk back into my pants and smiled like a

little bitch at the car as I neared his rolled-down window, saying something idiotic like, "I almost got piss on my pants!"

I at least expected a laugh from someone in his group, but it was too much to ask for a stupid white boy. The group kept quiet. Their demeanor didn't change at all.

I leaned against the banged-up side of the car and proceeded to ask, "Wassup? You good on sixty?"

I was new and not accustomed to multitasking and watching everything around me. I only barely paid attention as D lifted his arm up from his crotch. I reached out to grab what I was expecting to be a bag of weed, only to find he was holding a gun and pointing it right at me.

I immediately pulled my hand back, confused as hell. I'd given him zero reasons to fear me—I was never a threat, I always paid what I owed, and I was a little idiotic, but otherwise, the perfect customer.

My mind raced with how I was going to escape the situation, but I could hardly think. It was odd; if someone had pulled a gun on me while I was in uniform, I would've instantly reacted and made a thousand decisions in a fraction of a second. I was still a cop, but I was presenting myself as an addict, and that was all it took to erase my cop instincts in these situations. Staring down the barrel of a gun, I knew I was no longer in control. I took one step back and froze, waiting for him to make the decision on what I would do next.

"You tryin' to take my gun, nigga?" he asked.

I shook my head *no*. My biggest hope was that Kyle heard D and would call the SWAT team in.

He beckoned me closer, so I did as I was told. At the window, he instructed me to lean into him. This had moved me ten inches from the barrel to squarely align with it.

"Hey, man, I'm cool. You ain't gotta do this," I said.

I could have fought like I was trained, but my body chose not to. D ordered me to put my money in the car door handle just inside the window.

The SWAT team's coming . . . any second now, I told myself, reaching through the window.

Once he had my money, D lowered the gun to his thigh and pointed the weapon at a bag of marijuana between his legs.

"TAKE IT," he said, through gritted teeth.

I hesitated at first, but then quickly reached toward the dealer's crotch, grabbed the weed, and then shoved it into my pants pocket. D and his group made small comments, which I barely understood until I heard "PUSSY!" from the back seat.

I turned my back to them and stumbled to my car in disbelief. I slid into the driver's seat, pulled out my listening device, and repeated, "GUN!" about a dozen times as I dug out my police radio. I peered over at D and his group, who seemed to be waiting for me to leave before they did. Turning on my police radio, I continued to repeat "GUN" over and over. I let go of my mic, then turned up my walkie to await my instructions as I had zero idea what to do. No response. Kyle then chimed in and told me to meet him a few blocks over. I left the lot in total confusion.

Why the fuck aren't there a bunch of guys dressed in black uniforms swarming these guys? I wondered.

When I met up with Kyle, he told me something surprising. The SWAT team, which was dedicated to covering our squad's deals, had left the area to assist with the Gun Squad's surveillance. Every single one of them had fled the area. Not a single one had stayed to cover me in case something went wrong. Kyle later informed me that he'd approved the move. He, too, had underestimated D, which I couldn't be pissed about.

Kyle later apologized, stating he was glad I got the buy and that nothing else had gone wrong. He told me to look on the bright side. "Now we can prove D is known to be armed and give our SWAT team a leg up! They'll get a no-knock clause once they execute the search warrant on his home." But something *had* gone wrong. I had a gun pointed at me; at any second, D could have killed me. Still, I chose not to argue. I wanted to prove how tough I was and indicate that the dangers of the job were nothing to me. At that moment, I knew it was important to drive any fears of life-threatening scenarios deep down into my subconscious. If I could bury them, it was like they never happened.

I am just "the newbie." I am not the weak, shitty guy.

After the squad returned, and no one made a big deal of the incident, I chose to leave it behind me. I would be mentally stronger than the guy who had left the squad two years ago. I promised myself that if a gun were ever pointed in my face again, I would stare down its cold, metal barrel, unflinching.

There was a certain adrenaline rush that came with doing this job. For me, it was unlike any rush I'd ever felt. I would try to bring structure to one of the most unstructured and unpredictable environments in the world. This was a losing proposition. Obviously, I was new and had a skewed sense of how this work and world actually operated. But I also saw it as a challenge—each job gave me more of a rush. Every day, I knew I was going into a world that hated me because of who I worked for. Being found out would lead to an immediate and serious conflict. I was walking into the most dangerous parts of my city, where 90 percent of our murders and shootings occurred, more than half of them because of drug deals gone bad. I fed off of that negative energy and loved every bite. The more I did, the more I saw this as a competition between me and the bad guys and the more I got hooked. But also, the more I did, the less my brain and body reacted to the stimulus. I became accustomed to this level of adrenaline—I lived in it all day.

Even when I wasn't buying, I was hiding in the neighborhoods, surrounded by lookouts, gang members, and killers. I felt a constant rush, playing hide and seek in a real-world game. A game where losing meant death. As I continued to learn how to do my job, I trained myself to treat risk as if it were standard-issue equipment. My body began to associate greater risk with a greater high, and thus, a greater reward.

There was no real training that could teach me the correct way to build my undercover persona. So, I built Ricky with what felt good and right. I was trying to live as him in this dope world at work, then shut him off in my home life. The problem was, the line between these worlds was not as clear as I had thought. The more in-depth and difficult cases I got involved in, the further Ricky was pushed into my other life.

Looking back at who I was during my first few weeks, I don't even recognize that person. He seems like a stranger now. His natural instinct for self-preservation was intact, along with a healthy respect for danger and fear. I almost laugh at myself for having been so flooded with adrenaline and dopamine over something that I would do today and find utterly boring.

CHAPTER 4
STRIDE

Independence Avenue, known as "The Avenue," runs along the northeast side of Kansas City. It's a wasteland, a place forgotten by time itself.

Back in the day, the area housed much of the Italian mob, who focused on gambling, drug running, and out-of-sight prostitution. But a change in tides in the seventies mob war opened the door for a slow, creeping takeover. Now, it was home to those on the fringes—prostitutes, crack addicts, meth heads, and strung out, zombified tweakers who came here to live among their own kind.

Most people who walked The Avenue lived in low-income housing nearby, squatted in abandoned buildings, or camped in trash-filled alleyways in makeshift tents. They spent their days endlessly chasing their next fix, doing anything they needed to do to achieve that precious high. Though city officials knew it would be nearly impossible to clean up that section of town, they also knew they couldn't allow it to become a lawless faction of society. In hopes of putting a dent in the crime associated with the dope world, we were working to make as many arrests as we could, but throwing on the blue lights and driving up on clusters of people wasn't as effective as the more subtle approach. It was necessary to infiltrate these groups on their turf to curb the elements of crime that drugs were bringing to our city.

In this area, it was best to come off as someone completely non-threatening. Someone disheveled and even a little unhinged. I sure as shit looked the part. I had a ragged sweatshirt beneath my filthy Carhartt jacket. My jeans were torn and coated in motor oil, my shoes beat to shit with the soles half-fallen off. My hands were calloused, my nails packed with as much grime as I could scrape from puddles outside of the strip club. My hair was tangled and greasy from days of neglect.

Twenty minutes after the incident on Bales, I chewed the inside of my cheeks as Kyle navigated the bustling Kansas City streets, headed towards The Avenue. I stared through the windows as boutique stores and fancy restaurants gave way to dilapidated buildings with boarded-up windows, grimy liquor stores, and shops selling car parts and used tires.

Kyle cut the wheel when we reached Truman Road, then made a left on Paseo. It was below freezing outside with flakes of snow spitting from the sky as we drove past a 7-Eleven, a pawn shop, and a store that sold porn. As we stopped at a red light, I noticed two shivering individuals curled up inside a bus stop shelter beneath mounds of ripped, stained jackets; a group of boisterous women smiled and nodded their heads in our direction.

We took a right and circled back to The Avenue. That's when I spotted a group of several people huddled together on the corner.

"That them?" I asked.

Without a word, Kyle eased the car to a stop two blocks away on the opposite side of the street, just out of view. The group was comprised of three tall Black men in thick sweatshirts, one Black woman in skin-tight sweatpants and a dirty, fake fur jacket, and a white, blonde girl in dirty, black leggings with the word PINK across her ass in distressed ink and a stained, white puffer jacket. They were bunched together, their breath rising like puffs of smoke as they talked. As a beat-up Dodge Charger rumbled past, the Black woman broke free from the group and wandered toward the street, flashing a smile as she waved and hollered, "Hey, Baby! What you doin'?"

She opened her ragged jacket, revealing that she was braless beneath a paper-thin T-shirt; her low hanging breasts shook wildly at her every move. The car honked its horn but didn't stop. She gave them the middle finger and strutted back to the group, sidling up to the girl in the white jacket. I squinted and noticed the tallest man in the group reaching into his pocket. I could just make out a broken glass straw; his head was on a swivel as he began to pack the makeshift pipe.

"Hurry the fuck up, dude," I said. "Just let me out before you start pointing at them too."

"Okay, settle down, son." Kyle raised his eyebrows as he pulled out of the spot and drove two blocks north. He pulled the car over next to two overflowing trash cans outside an apartment with bars on the windows; a scrawny pit bull grabbed a discarded chicken bone from the asphalt and darted into the nearest alleyway. The car door let out a cold creek as I opened it and stepped out into the biting air.

"When you're done, Kelly will be waiting for you at the Shady Lady," Kyle called.

"All right," I said. "If this doesn't work out, I'll keep walking 'til the next group."

"Try not to fuck this up," he said with a nod.

I rolled my eyes and shook my head. Just as I stooped down to close the door, he called out, "Hey, Ricky?"

"Yeah?"

"You smell like shit."

"Love you too, Dad," I replied with a smirk.

I slammed the door shut and kept my head down as I ducked into an alleyway to go over my plan. As I'd learned on Bales, a white guy walking up to a group cold like this always raised a red flag. I'd need to find a way in that didn't involve me sauntering up to them and fucking up the scene.

I knew I could do this, but I had to step up my game and try to lose my police identity—and quick.

My buy money was tucked into an envelope, which I had hidden in my left sock. I pulled out the crisp bills, spit into my palms and rubbed the bills until the edges curled before tossing them on the ground and grinding them down with the tip of my shoe. Then, I picked them up and shoved them into my left pocket.

Go time.

Drawing a deep breath, I stepped out of the alley, making

a left, then a right. When I hit The Avenue, I stumbled onto the street about 100 yards from the group I'd spotted from the car. A cop certainly couldn't drink on the job, but I was allowed to while I was undercover. So, I shoved my hands into my pockets and ducked into a nearby liquor store. I grabbed a tallboy can of malt liquor from a barely cold cooler with faded Busch stickers on its doors. The store smelled like cat piss and incense, and when the guy behind the counter told me what I owed, I grumbled and swayed a little, so I looked like I was already drunk. I threw a dollar bill onto the counter, along with some nickels and pennies for the rest, then swiped the paper bag with the can in it, rolled the bag down over the sides, and cracked it as I stepped back outside. I sipped the beer and allowed my fingers to trace the cigarette pack that Kelly had given me in my right pocket, still grateful for her advice.

The group was still huddled tightly but had moved next to the side door of an abandoned grocery store. I had to get their attention somehow; anything that could let their guard down once I wedged my way into their group. If they noticed me first and thought I was just some crazy guy, they wouldn't see me as a threat when I forced my way into their circle. But to do this, I had to commit to looking completely apathetic.

I gutted down a long sip of the beer, nearly puking up foam, and jogged across a side street, scanning the ground for cigarette butts, pieces of metal, really anything I could possibly pick up. Once I was directly across from the group, I walked to the edge of the sidewalk and gritted my teeth. Despite the cars whizzing past, I walked right into the speeding traffic, almost daring them to hit me. Drivers laid on their horns as cars barely hit their brakes and swerved around me, but I didn't flinch. Instead, I chugged the last of the beer, crushed the can in my fist, and threw it at the exhaust pipe of a dented sedan as it flew past. It missed—thank God.

Heads in the group were turning; just what I wanted.

I trained my eyes directly ahead, making my way to the doorway of a Mexican restaurant less than ten yards from where they stood. I stepped to the left of the restaurant's open door, unzipped my pants, and began to pee on the wall right next to a menu featuring blown out photos of rice and beans. As my steaming urine hit the wall and slid down the dank sidewalk, the restaurant owner flew through the door, screaming something in Spanish.

"Fuck you!" I screamed back. I finished peeing and stumbled backwards, leaving my fly open. "Fuck YOU, motherfucker!" I intentionally let spit fly out of my mouth and it dripped down my beard as I yelled, "Fucking idiots!"

I continued scanning the sidewalk as I stumbled, noticing the group beginning to laugh and jeer. Still yelling nonsense, I stooped down and swiped a cigarette butt from the ground near the spot where my piss was pooling. I shoved it into my coat pocket, then wandered over to the group.

I swayed closer to them and rasped, "Who got a light?"

Now that I was close, they got quiet—the men took a step back.

The tension broke as I reached into my pocket and produced a ratty, nearly empty pack of Pall Malls, and put one in my mouth. "I got another stick if someone has a light," I said. I was working in a stutter now.

Most of the group took small steps back, watching me through narrowed eyes. Finally, the prostitute in the white puffer reached into her bra and pulled out a clear purple lighter with a peeling heart sticker on it. As I put the small butts I picked up from the ground into my now empty pack, I casually fumbled with a small crack pipe that I'd made out of an old piece of a retractable car antenna—I'd even singed the end on a candle at home. I took the lighter from the blonde girl and put an extra cigarette in my mouth, lighting them both. As I handed her the smoke, I noticed her nails were broken; a couple so short that they were bleeding. She put the cigarette between her rotten teeth and exhaled a big puff of smoke. Smoking was seemingly simple, but I had never smoked a cigarette in my life. So, I concentrated hard on trying to mimic her every move and unfucked myself before the group noticed, as I was holding my cigarette like some actress from the 1940s movies my grandma used to make me watch.

"Hey, Mama, mind if I keep this?" I asked, still holding onto her lighter.

Her bloodshot eyes widened as she scratched at an open sore on her face. One of the guys stepped closer as she rubbed at her red-rimmed eyes and replied, "For $2 you can."

"Lemme keep it and I'll hook you up." I noticed a bottle cap on the ground, picked it up, and shoved it into my pocket.

She stared back at me, continuing to pick at her face until a pinprick of blood appeared on the biggest sore. She shook her head and put her hand out.

"Come on. You know what's up. Listen, I got twenty and

I'm not looking to screw. Help me out, and I got you, girl. I ain't even tryin' to get my dick sucked, know what I mean?"

At the sight of money and the mention of a hookup, the group started to scramble over to me. I wasn't a threat anymore—I was a means to a hit of some good shit. I sucked down the Pall Mall as group members started to leer, "Come on young'n, I got you. Let me call my guy."

"I got him first," the prostitute spat, pulling my arm. "My guy's shit is fire!"

Up until this point, I felt no nerves; it almost felt normal to be in this element. But now that she was walking me into the alley with the sole purpose of buying crack, I began to get anxious. There was a sense of fear, but it wasn't out of any perceived danger. My mind was racing with all kinds of things to say, expecting to be grilled by the dealer who would soon show up. The adrenaline was roaring through my body, my ears got hot, and my hands shook uncontrollably. I had to bite my lip just to keep it from shaking. This part of society, constantly engaging on the other side of the law, was so foreign to me that my body was trying to keep up with what I was forcing myself into.

I followed my new friend into the alleyway, which smelled like human shit. The ground was littered with piles of feces, bags of trash, and mountains of shingles spilling from a nearby dumpster. Out of the corner of my eye, I noticed two screws on the ground, bent down, and grabbed them. The prostitute adjusted her pants and pulled a cracked flip phone from her waistband. She opened it and fired off a text. "I need the money," she said, reaching her hand out.

"Shiiiiit," I replied, shaking my head.

"My dude ain't gonna meet someone new. I need your money," she said, stepping towards me.

"Guess I'll just go get it from the dude over there," I said, pointing to one of the other guys from the group.

"He ain't gonna deal with a white dude. You gotta give me your money." She brushed at her stringy blond hair with her ragged nails, her eyes wild. "It's all cool, just give me the fuckin' money!"

It would have been easy to hand her the cash, but I knew that if she bought the crack, she'd hide it in her crotch and run. "I ain't some pup. You go get it and bring it here, or I'll get with someone else!"

"Just give me the goddamn money! Dude's almost here. The shit is literally right here."

I paced back and forth, stumbled a little, then looked her in the eyes. "Nah, nah, Mama. You can tell your boy I'm gone."

She narrowed her eyes as she opened her phone and sent another text. I scanned the ground again and stumbled, my foot slipping into a fresh pile of shit. I bent down and picked up an old pen cap and a washer caked in grime. That's when a large, Black man rounded the corner in a blue puffer jacket and heavily stained, ripped jeans—the dope man. Clearly, he was just a runner for the real dealer—just a pawn in the dope game. He walked towards us with purpose, glaring at me. "A fuckin' white guy?"

"He's cool," the prostitute called out, raising her hands. "He's cool, he's cool."

The dope man looked me up and down.

"He's my boy. I've worked with him, know what I mean?

He's good," she said, placing a hand on his shoulder. I was shocked. I didn't have to do any of the talking, she just took over. She was smooth and confident, brushing off any concerns about the stranger that I was with such ease. This is what it looked like to live this, not just make it a role. This is exactly what I would have to do, and why it was key to be placed into this situation and do it hundreds of times.

The only way to learn how to be like this woman was to be around her and allow myself to convert into a similar version of her. What I learned from her made the biggest impact on me and may well have been the start of my downfall. To be successful, this was not some role or something I could just turn on and off, any more than she could. This started my transformation into Ricky, which could only be made possible with the loss of Brent.

"What you trying to do?" he asked, puffing his chest.

I got a confidence boost from her and immediately belted out like some veteran, "I got twenty."

The dope man stared at me for a minute, his eyes scanning my face, then landing on my shit-caked shoes. He smirked, revealing rows of brown, broken teeth. He quickly worked his index finger into his mouth and pulled a rock packaged in a knotted plastic baggie out of his cheek, then placed it in his palm.

I looked at it and shook my head. "Nah, man. I need two of 'em," I said, pulling out the dirty, damp cash.

He dug his fingers back into his mouth and pulled out a second small crack rock, this one covered in green mucus. I put my hand out and didn't flinch as he took the twenty and slid the tiny wet wads into my hand. He pocketed the money and watched me fumble with my score. He stepped forward, dropping his guard. "Hey, little man," he said, putting his arm around me and pulling me into his smoke-laden jacket. "Go ahead and load that up and lemme get a pull."

This was a pivotal moment—now everyone would want a free hit. They'd soon start wandering up from all sides. "Yeah, yeah. Hold on a minute," I slurred.

The dope man squeezed my neck in the crook of his arm and leaned in so close I could smell the cheap vodka on his breath. He placed his cold cheek against mine, "You're gonna love this; it's fire."

"Yeah, and you owe me," the girl said, stepping forward.

"Hang on, hang—hang on," I said, shoving the rocks into my pocket.

"C'mon, homie," the dope man said.

With his arm still locked around my neck, I worked my hand into my pocket. Using my nails, I pulled the plastic knot off of one of the baggies, put it into my palm, and slid it into the Dope Man's hand. Thinking it was a piece of the crack, he loosened his grip and smirked. Without hesitation, I ducked and ran just as he looked down at the knot and yelled, "Hey, motherfucker!"

The two started to chase me as I sprinted out of the alley, holding my baggy pants up as I made my way onto the street.

The girl shrieked, "You owe me, fucker!"

"Get the FUCK back here!" the dope man shouted.

My heart slammed my ribs as I raced down the street and made a quick left, nearly running into a chain link fence. All chain link fences on this side of town were installed upside down, razor-sharp metal sticking out of the top. I tucked my hands into the jacket to give me some padding—I didn't have time to hesitate, so I threw myself over the fence, my body dropping into a muddy backyard. I had to be careful; most of these yards housed angry dogs, and the ground was riddled with rusty metal and old needles. I had to move—if they caught me, they'd beat me to shit before I could call for help, and a group of pissed off crackheads could do some serious fucking damage.

I threw myself over another fence, bolted down an alleyway, and sprinted down a side street, slipping in another pile of human shit. I ducked between houses, cut through a parking lot, then tucked myself behind a dumpster until I was sure I had lost them. Still desperately holding my baggy jeans up, I made it another quarter-mile before my feet hit Chestnut, and Kelly's minivan in the strip club parking lot came into view. I pumped my arms as I bolted toward it, then yanked the door open and launched myself into the passenger seat.

"Was it a good run?" she asked, eyes twinkling with amusement. I could do nothing but burst into laughter. I smelled like shit and piss, cheap booze and cigarettes, and I was high on something better than the rocks in my pocket. I pushed my filthy hair out of my face, fumbled for Kelly's radio, pressed the button on the side, and spat, "Good deal. I'm off the block."

The radio crackled; Kyle responded, "What the fuck was that man?"

I tossed the radio onto the floor, let out another hysterical laugh, and gave Kelly a firm nod as she peeled out of the neighborhood.

I shocked my new boss and my new squad with my success, but I also annoyed them by telling them every minor detail of the buy. They had been buying for years—what I'd just done was no big deal. However, I was like a kid who had jumped on a bike and ridden by myself for the first time. The sensation was exhilarating, and it hadn't even been a difficult or crazy buy. As my career progressed, a buy like this wouldn't even raise my heart rate. But, for now, it was rocking me. I couldn't wait to tell anyone who would listen and do it all again. They were unimpressed, and now I can't blame them. I was just beginning to learn to crawl.

In my first three months of working undercover, I learned the power of adaptation: how most of the deals we make in life and our methods of survival are just a combination of body language, creative props, and methods of mimicking. My squad was made up of master chameleons. Though most of them were burned out, emotionally jaded, and had no lives outside of the job, the majority of us found that work was—ironically—one of the only places we could show our darkest, shadiest, shittiest selves. Somehow, the peculiar authenticity we found in inauthenticity was something we deeply valued.

On the flip side, I found it absolutely fucking insane that I could potentially see my coworkers out in the real world someday—shopping at the grocery store, out in lawn chairs at the Kansas City Parade, or lining the bleachers of a little league baseball game—and I would likely not even recognize them. They'd have names I wouldn't associate with them, families they'd rarely spoken about, and they'd wear clean clothes. It made me think about how deep the fabrications went: how many of the traits they displayed on the job came naturally to them, and which were far more pretend.

In truth, I'd created Ricky out of a template of someone I *kind of* wanted to be—only to discover that this wildcard persona had been living inside of me the entire time. In some ways, Ricky was innate, and yet, observing how the squad approached their work made me all the more skilled at developing him. Each person on our team had unique superpowers, and those strengths refined mine.

The entire group seeded a twinkling inspiration in everything I saw. I'd be barreling down the interstate, then suddenly feel compelled to stop and examine a ball of chicken wire, cardboard boxes, or aluminum cans on the side of the road. If there's one thing the houseless community taught me, it's that anything discarded could be useful when building a life, especially things that were unique to Ricky— his favorite fast food, drinks, and candy bars (the wrappers of which I was constantly scooping up to tuck away in the seams of my vehicle).

I certainly had no interest in housing thousands of extra calories per day just to play the part. (I mean, let's face it, I was already putting my life and health in enough danger.) So, I'd eye every craft beer can I saw, considering how it'd look in the shrine of my car. After about six weeks, things like used toothpicks, wadded Kleenexes, and bottles of piss that rolled around in my floorboard after having to take a leak on a surveillance were practically mementos. I'd even come to love the odor of the job: the smell of piss, shit, cigarette smoke, motor oil, and night right before it touches morning. All of it began to represent a private, cutthroat thrill inside of me: a shadowy ambition I could not shake and a silly motherfucker who was up for literally anything.

I was constantly surprising myself and Kyle with my ingenious stunts that worked out to our benefit. One of my favorites stemmed from the day I found a large, triangular Domino's Pizza delivery topper in the median of the interstate. I cracked into it and rigged a flashlight to sit inside it to give it the authentic glow. I guessed that it had probably fallen off of someone's delivery car, which meant it was fair game for my undercover use. In search of an old Domino's employee shirt, I hit up several thrift stores until I found one (my lucky day). Suddenly, I was Ricky the Pizza Guy—which was fucking genius, even if Kyle didn't wildly praise it in the beginning. The opportunity I saw for "delivering pizzas" had to do with the search warrants for dope dealers' houses. Before we executed a search warrant, it was imperative to know they were home, and to do so without them knowing our undercover had set them up. I would show up to our target house and knock away.

Once the door was answered, I could immediately launch into an annoyed, "Large pepperoni comes to $14.87."

Most of the time, whoever was in the house would be confused. They might say something like, "I didn't order no fucking pizza," which would create room for me to "apologize for my confusion."

"Damn. This ain't 4904 Garfield? Oh! My bad, dude, is this Brooklyn? I'm one block over. My bad."

Once I could confirm either speaking with the dealer or

eyeballing him in the home, I could go back to my car, send a signal over the radio, and get our SWAT team there to kick the door in. (Yes, all because some Domino's driver lost their topper on the side of the road.) Shit would just pan out like that sometimes, and it kept me using props and creativity to further slip into my role, which just hooked me on the job even more.

Who here's the dope fiend? I'd think, completely intoxicated by all things Ricky. The thing is, this trait wasn't mine alone. I saw it in every single detective we had. In some ways, it was infectious.

The more dangerous experiences I had, the more I craved them. When I was home and *separate* from Ricky, I found a strange loneliness creeping in, like the people who knew me didn't really know me at all.

This made it challenging to share my world with Wesley because I'd only talk to her about the easy and mundane tasks I completed at work. That way, I'd shield her from the brutalities of what was true. She would panic if she knew that I was scrounging through the piss and shit in back alleyways while arguing with crack dealers over their prices, patting crack rocks down in my jacket pockets for safekeeping and allowing drug fiends with pistols into the front seat of my car. It would be even more troubling for her to know that these were the things that kept me on cloud nine and going back for more every day.

When I wasn't buying things from Goodwill or the Salvation Army, I was nabbing discarded things out of homeless camps. As a new white undercover, a huge aspect of the job was pretending to be a mostly homeless addict and looking like complete dogshit. People on the streets were sharp, and they knew their kind. The more they were around you, the more they'd start to pick up on the little visual things: the fact that your clothes fit too well, the fact that you didn't have lots of bruises and scabs, or if you weren't constantly itching.

Unfortunately, they were also largely aware of your teeth, and dental health was not something I was willing to compromise, so I bought enamel paint from a costume store that made my shit looked caked with nicotine yellow. I never got used to seeing myself in the mirror; it was always an equally disgusting and satisfying view. In the evenings, after I stripped down to nothing, my dogs would encircle me and begin scratching at my legs, panting and wagging their tails wildly. I loved the notion that, despite the many layers of filth that covered my body, they always knew who I was and weren't too inconvenienced to remind me.

And, of course, Wesley was never inconvenienced either. She loved seeing me happy, and it didn't really matter what I was up to as long as I was content. And within three months of me going undercover, we became especially happy together—overjoyed by the news of our pregnancy with our second child.

CHAPTER 5
SUPER 8

Kansas City in July is a furnace—the air is thick and oppressive. My shitty air conditioner was no match for the 100-degree heat, which always left me drenched in sweat within seconds of entering the driver's seat. All around me, hobos seemed to go unchanged by the shifting of the seasons; no weather conditions would slow their almighty addiction, desperation, and compulsion for more.

As an undercover, I had become familiar with the heavily trafficked pockets of the city where addicts loved to tuck themselves away to smoke crack, get drunk, and scheme ways to con the unsuspecting. They particularly loved to camp out in roach-infested motels in the crotch and armpit areas of the city, setting up their little narcotics bodegas that reeked of piss, wet dog, and dank sweat.

My squad focused on the desperate dealers in society—those who used and sold an ounce or less. These are the most unpredictable kinds of dope deals and the most likely to end in violence. The big dope deals with the cartel or high-level dealers were more business-like, and I found them less stressful than buying a car. Most of my dealers were wanderers who had been kicked out of family members', friends', or acquaintances' homes, which seemed reasonable to me, as these types of addicts were some of the least trustworthy people on the planet. Their addiction prevented them from having boundaries, so they would rob, steal, kill, and do vile things for their next sale or rip someone off in order to get their next hit.

I'd been in the business long enough to know—those who try to help these junkies almost always get burned. In best-case scenarios, they'd have their valuables lifted or have law enforcement "kick them in" (street slang for having a search warrant executed on your house); in worst case scenarios, well-intended loved ones would be blackmailed or murdered, especially if a deal went bad.

Suffice it to say, the grimiest motels in the city get a lot of traffic: drug lords, sellers, buyers, and internet prostitutes who use the rooms to funnel clients.

The preferred hideouts are motels with doors hidden from view, peepholes being a bonus to spot trouble and escape quickly. Their fear of the police is second to the fear of being robbed or killed for their dope stash by the very people they surround themselves with. The scary part of this is, they don't fear being killed nearly as much as being robbed. The rooms are almost impossible to get into unless you've got a modicum of "street cred" or some trusted doper has some kind of loyalty to you.

As Ricky, I had been on the job less than a year. I was

shedding the last of my engrained police habits. Drug users were highly skeptical of me, but that was largely because I was white. All white guys were assumed to be the police in the hood. It'd taken me at least six months before Ricky's personality felt more developed and real rather than rehearsed. As for the part of me that remained—Brent—he existed less and less as work shifts in the drug-addled world added up, as did the hours I spent hanging out with people from society's seedy underbelly.

At about eight months in, though, things started to shift: I'd cut my teeth calling dealers, buying drugs in the front seat of my work vehicle, knocking on doors, and talking my way into complete strangers' homes, and I earned my first informant—or "snitch"—depending on how you look at it.

I met this informant in a Target parking lot on the nicer side of Kansas City. The plan was simple: we'd meet, talk about how we'd work together, and set ground rules. Most of the time, these informants were covered in pockmarks from meth use. Have you ever had a bug on you and been tricked by your body into thinking you had hundreds more that you could feel but couldn't see? A similar sensation is a side effect of meth use—users constantly pick and scratch at their body until bloody scabs develop. They begin to reorder their priorities; hygiene is the first to go. This causes these sores to fester for months, becoming swollen, red, and crusty.

"Just don't get too lax, man," Kyle warned. "Can't trust these fucks as far as you can throw 'em. At the end of the day —they're still criminals."

I'd come to understand that the hours melded together on the streets and only cops were on time, so I needed to be a little late to everything. We'd agreed to meet in the Target parking lot at noon, so I rolled into the parking lot around 12:45 p.m. I waited for over an hour before accepting that I'd been stood up and subsequently drove back to the office. At 4 p.m., I caught a phone call from my informant asking where I was. Frustrated, I drove back to the Target and picked her up anyway. She was a tired-looking woman with matted hair and bloodshot eyes, wearing skin-tight leggings and an ill-fitting tank top. She slid into the passenger seat with zero hesitation, completely unfazed by the fact that she was several hours late. I just let it ride.

We planned to roll out to meet some dealers who my informant had called without me, something I had warned against. This was all too common—following the rules was almost an impossibility in this realm. I spent the next couple of hours conducting a half-dozen buys without any effort—it was so easy, it felt like cheating. Every buy went off without a hitch, and I met my weekly stat goal within those two hours. Each buy I did was a felony case, which would have the dealer's door kicked in by my SWAT team, who would take their dope, money, and guns. This meant I could be the victor in this game.

I was almost out of money when my informant made a call to a guy named Joey. She picked at her face as she spoke to him in a low voice, agreeing that we'd meet him at the shitty $49 a night motel where he was staying. These phone calls and conversations were oddly quick and uncomplicated. Sometimes we'd talk in code to make our intentions known; other times we would just flat out say, "Can I meet up with you? I need fifty," referring to $50 worth of whatever dope this dealer specialized in.

"Let's get it," I said, as she hung up. "He living at this motel?"

"Yeah," my informant said, adjusting her vent. "He got kicked out of his momma's house for selling meth and pawning a bunch of her shit."

"Sounds about right," I responded.

We quickly turned out of the parking lot, headed to a Super 8 near a large truck stop on the outskirts of town. We'd told Joey we'd be at his room by 6:30 p.m., so I made a point to drive as slowly as possible, taking a few wrong turns along the way, burning a couple of Newports with my raggedy ride along to kill time.

My shitty tires squealed into the parking lot of the horseshoe-shaped Super 8 with all the doors hidden from peering passers-by. I eyed the five or six empty cars scattered throughout the lot as I made a pass to find the second-floor room Joey had told us to go to. With so few cars in the area, the surveillance detectives would have a hard time parking close to keep watch over me; I knew I would have to rely solely on my early 2000s Nokia brick phone for audio surveillance. The phone acted as a one-way listening apparatus. My team could hear me, and that was it—but to say that they could really *hear* is not entirely accurate. The audio was mostly garbled speech with a few laughs tied in.

My informant and I sat silently for a few seconds as I reached down to peel my sweat-soaked T-shirt off my body, making it blatantly obvious that I was not armed and that my small stature was non-threatening. As we clambered up the cement and iron stairs to room 204, adrenaline coursed through my veins.

For the average person, the brain dumps a rush of adrenaline as a reflex for the fear of the unknown and the danger they are about to encounter. This primal instinct heightens their senses so they can react, escape, and survive the threats they're facing. I had overridden this instinct as a way to be able to do this job; it was the only way I was able to get myself into the dangerous areas this role demanded. I had no choice. I had to do this work and do it the only way I knew how—all-in. The interesting part was that I began to experience this build up as a flush of energy that hit more like excitement. This was straight dopamine, ten times stronger than anything I'd ever known. And it sparked a desire to chase the thrill over and over.

The concrete of the balcony vibrated under our feet as we moved. We neared our destination where Joey cracked the door open for us, his body blocking the other side. He peeled it open just far enough for us to slip inside the grimy room with two beds, a TV, a sticky, peeling 1970s hutch, a small nook that acted as a closet, and a tiny bathroom with a flickering halogen light in the back. As with any buy inside a home or motel, my eyes traced the surfaces of the room—tables, beds, desk—to take in the entire situation in a matter of a single second so as not to throw alarm. My eyes caught the silhouette of an assault rifle and a green bulletproof vest leaning against the wall in the furthest corner of the room. I was there for meth but had just set my sights on an even better prize. I carefully shifted my gaze to try to distinguish other weapons but didn't see any. Suddenly, the door slammed behind me causing my body to rock forward and my head to duck.

"Motherfucker's out there just sittin' in the parking lot," Joey bellowed, migrating away from the door.

This behavior wasn't unusual for someone on meth—the paranoia is intense, so all-consuming that it rattles their bones. It drives reckless decisions without any concept of repercussions for their actions. Joey's comment sparked my immediate worry that Kyle could be out there; he was the only one of our group who would choose to park this close. I could easily picture him waiting out in the barren lot—in plain sight. I casually reached into my pocket for the Nokia I'd use to cue my team that someone was spooking my dealer.

"Where he at? Want me to go fuck 'em up?" I asked, peering out the filthy window to see if he'd point out the car.

Joey lurched back towards the door, opened it a crack, and I peeked through, squinting to see a shitty red Mazda convertible from the early 2000s. Not Kyle. Just some skeezy old man waiting on a hooker. Joey forced the door shut once more, then sat on the bed to start our sale. He pulled a clear plastic bag from his pocket; I could see without further examination that it was meth. I took the dope and paid him with barely any discussion—once again, another easy buy for the day.

Then, my eyes fell back on the gun and the vest in the corner. Here's the deal—if there was something illegal that I could buy, I was going to try for it. Just as meth heads couldn't control their paranoia, I couldn't control my compulsion to say yes to this. There was no just leaving it be. If pressed, I would tell you that I knew a gun buy would be huge—way more impactful than a tiny bag of meth. Add in my competitive drive and it was like rocket fuel. I didn't give a shit that buying a gun in a shitty Super 8 was dangerous as fuck.

"What about that?" I said, nodding at the rifle. "How much you want for that?"

Joey's eyebrows lifted, and he rounded the bed, walked toward the gun, and held it up, examining it.

"How bad you want it?" he began. "$300?"

"How bout two?" I replied. We settled on $250, and I asked Joey to hold the gun for me, explaining that I needed to do a few break-ins to get the cash, but I'd be back in a few hours. After he agreed, my informant and I walked out of the motel and back down to my car feeling invigorated that everything had gone smoothly and that I was about to add a gun buy to my week. (An idiotic false sense of security.)

My informant and I climbed back into my shithole van, leaving the motel behind. Before I dropped her off, I warned her to hold tight (to not get high and disappear, in case I needed her later). I called my sergeant, who happened to be Deb from my patrol days, and explained everything. While she was pleased with the buy, I had to talk her into letting us go back to the motel, since it was late in our workday and we were up against infuriating and pedantic new policies about reducing overtime. I knew being told no would feel like losing to Joey, so I negotiated the conditions needed to get the go-ahead—even if one of those conditions was doing it with a smaller cover team.

"It'll be a quick and easy buy," I swore. "I just need one

detective to listen in and a few SWAT guys to cover me. I've got control of this dude. I'll be in and out quick."

Deb reluctantly agreed. Before heading back to the Super 8, I darted over to my office to pick up more cash and scan through police reports involving Joey. My heart was racing. Part of me worried about how much time this was all taking, but then I remembered that addicts give zero fucks about the clock. After several minutes of research, I learned that Joey was the main suspect in a series of police car break-ins and had stolen several assault rifles, handguns, and bulletproof vests. The more I read, the more personal it felt; a wave of competitiveness surged through my bones. I wasn't going to let this motherfucker continue to walk as a free man. I would not be satisfied with just the rifle. This was a nagging urge. I would take *any* risk to get every gun back and have him pay for fucking with my tribe. All of this fueled my addiction to this game, which continued in a vicious cycle.

As I waited for my surveillance detective to get in place, I received a call from my informant. "Joey's high as fuck now and he's paranoid as shit. He's called me thirty-six fucking times. He'll only sell the gun to you if I come too," she stated.

I agreed to pick her up, though I was actually pissed since I wanted to distance my informant from this buy. I didn't want her getting caught in the middle if things went south. But more importantly, I didn't want her suffering the consequences on the streets if it was known she'd brought a cop into the group. Nevertheless, I scooped her up and found myself parking in the same spot just below Joey's room.

Joey physically gripped my shirt and pulled me inside the motel room as my informant shuffled in on my heels. This time, the space was dark, muggy, and stank with body heat from a small crowd that had gathered. One guy and two women scowled from the first bed as I walked in. Their pinhole pupils, thousand-yard stare, and twitching movements made me sure they'd been smoking meth for days. I'd been around enough tweakers to know they were observing me with unrivaled hypervigilance. Using meant going for days without sleep, becoming paranoid, agitated, impulsive, and, like all addicts, becoming a myopic, in-the-moment thinker. This type of drug user had no care. Their thoughts existed in the moment—usually their dope stash and money—but they didn't care about the long-term consequences.

A large bag of meth sat on the nightstand between the two unmade beds, and all eyes were on me as everyone acted like guard dogs protecting their stash. The youngest woman stood and walked to the far corner, making phone calls, working to move the dope. Brent would have felt prickling nerves, but I was Ricky, and I was riding a certain cockiness that had become chronic in my nature. Conversations quieted to whispers as Joey walked me to the back of the room where the gun still leaned against the wall. I picked it up, pretending I didn't know how it worked, though it was a weapon whose mechanisms I had memorized after two decades of military and police work. The sleek, black silhouette, the curved magazine, and the snarling barrel stared back at me. I knew I was to grasp the grip with my fingers curled and with my thumb ready to engage. I should nestle the stock against my shoulder and take aim. Yet, I pushed all that aside and did what Ricky would do. I put my finger on the trigger and waved it around the room, pointing it at everyone. I went as far as acting like I would put it in my waistband as if it were a handgun to help prove I was just some idiot and not a cop. Just as simple and easy as the meth buy from earlier, I paid Joey for the gun. It was now mine, and so was his ass.

I knew so many things could be done with what I had already accomplished. Cases could be created, a search warrant written up, arrests could be made, and detective work could build upon it to make the case even bigger. Unfortunately, my competitive nature demanded that I do more in the moment. So, surrounded by the most unpredictable people, I made a split-second decision to keep pushing. No quick in-and-out like I promised Deb. I wasn't free to leave until I bought everything and arranged to buy whatever else Joey had stashed elsewhere. That led me to ask for the bulletproof vest I'd seen earlier.

"You're too late, man. Someone beat you to it."

My attention was quickly pulled towards the small door that closed off the toilet and shower. A skinny guy with veins popping from his lean physique had thrown the door open wildly. As he stepped out, I could make out his baggy shorts, no shirt, and, of course, the bulletproof vest.

"Sorry, bro," Joey immediately stated. "He had the cash."

Though I was frustrated, I didn't show it; it was just part of the game, and it felt like a loss. Since I couldn't have that, I reached harder.

I looked back to the guy in the vest, whose eyes were wild, filled with agitation, impulsivity, and unpredictability. It was a look that oddly held my attention—like my brain was telling me to register the underlying emotion and predict the danger that was about to go down; to give me just a split second of a head start to make my move.

"C'mon, motherfucker! Let's see how this shit works! SHOOT ME!" the guy in the vest yelled in my direction, nodding as I held onto my score.

"Nah, man. I think this shit would smoke that vest," I replied. This idiot was lucky I knew better. That vest would do nothing to protect his ass with this caliber of a weapon.

My attention pinged back and forth between the vest guy, who kept begging me to shoot him, and the quick movements happening around the room. By that point, my informant had taken a seat on the bed and was looking at a handgun with the older woman. I knew that if it were for sale, she would help facilitate that deal, so I ignored her and let her work.

Having lost most of my cop instincts, I blocked out the entire room and locked Joey into a one-on-one conversation. "You ever get anything smaller, like a nine? I got the cash, and I need something more mobile. Ya feel me?"

"I've got access to lots of handguns," Joey bragged. "Give me a day or so and I'll get you whatever you want."

As we worked on what kinds of guns he could get me, I lost focus and quit tracking everyone in the room. Then, I felt it, that human instinct that warns you someone is right behind you.

My reflexes took over, and I whirled around, only to find myself face-to-face with the man who had previously been watching me from the bed, his expression eerily darkened. I stayed calm, ignoring the warning signs that my brain was picking up on.

"Hey, man, what's up?" I said, smiling, though my voice was much lower than I'd intended. I'd barely blinked, and before I knew it, I found myself with a black revolver pressed against my forehead. I froze in shock; I felt the blood leave my head and rush into my body as the room swirled in liquid motion.

"Why you askin' so many questions, motherfucker? Who the fuck are you?"

I was so caught off guard that I couldn't utter a word.

He pressed the gun harder into my head. I held my breath, blinking furiously as his rancid breath made my nostrils flare; the inflamed capillaries in his eyes made him look all the more unpredictable and desperate to take control of me . . . of the situation itself.

Dissatisfied with my inability to answer, he pushed me backward through the bathroom door. There, he snatched my shirt and shoved me down. I tried to catch myself on the slimy toilet, but I missed and slipped, falling inside the gritty, yellowed bathtub. He towered over me, sneering, arm outstretched, gripping the gun that hovered over my eyes, allowing me to see the white in his knuckles as he maintained a death grip on the handle. As I looked up, all I could do was count the bullets inside the cylinder of the revolver. There was a bullet in each and every hole.

I stared into the eyes of my executioner, jamming my sweat-soaked palms into the sides of the enamel bathtub to maneuver my head away from the inevitable bullet. My limbs were spread wide, leaving my stomach vulnerable; my neck jammed into the metal drain plug, causing the nerves in my neck to send radiating pain to my head. My stare didn't break with the man who peered into me, and all I saw was the intense enjoyment he took from my vulnerability. With each second, he grew more enraged that I'd defied his questioning, but the honest truth is, I just couldn't answer. I watched his finger press against the trigger, and I knew that even the smallest flinch would cause his gun to fire.

I tried to move my head away from the barrel, but he drove it even harder into my skin, forcing my head back. All of my training told me to grab the gun and fight for it, but in that moment, it was as if I'd received no training at all. The guy in the vest barged into the tiny bathroom, drawn in by the voyeuristic drive to watch my death. He leaned forward and yanked the shower curtain around us, using it as a shield to mitigate the inevitable blood splatter. With the curtain in place, he began begging the man to shoot me. It almost seemed like he was taunting him, as if he *couldn't* do it. All the while, my oblivious SWAT team and backup detective were parked less than a minute away, listening to the usual static and inaudible noise from my listening device. They might as well have been at home, watching TV on the couch.

I lay there, powerless. Of all the times in my career that I'd had to fight for my life, this was the first time that I had nothing. My brain seemed to completely shut down.

I choked on spit and couldn't speak as the questions kept coming.

"Who the fuck are you? Why the fuck are you *really* here?"

All I could do was absorb what were surely my last moments alive. Joey appeared over the man's shoulder with an emotionless stare. It was clear that I was not being viewed as a human being. I hoped that desperately looking them in the eyes would somehow humanize me. There was no confusing me with a cop at that moment; my animal body had defaulted to helplessness. I was just a man dressed in the identity of another man, about to die in a Super 8 bathroom. This wasn't even the worst part of town. My wife was at our home less than ten minutes away, probably settling in after putting our daughter to bed.

For the first time on the job, I believed my death was inevitable. I was going out at the hand of a busted-up junkie, and I didn't even know why. All my hopes of leaving the room alive had eroded, until an unlikely comrade came into view.

My informant.

Though Joey pulled at her to stop her, he couldn't restrain her from pulling the man with the gun off me and yelling at him to knock this shit off as she stepped between us. This woman was risking her life for me—she, who I had been warned I could not trust and who I had known for less than a day. Her instinct chose to fight in that moment as mine had chosen freeze. She could have easily done nothing or simply ran away, leaving me behind. Either of those would have made sense for who I thought she was as a person. She was a criminal and a meth addict, which in this world meant that I could not rely on her. But that day, *she fucking came through.* I never expected her to actually save my life.

Unbelievably, this distracted the man from his efforts; he lowered the weapon, then extended his arm, prompting me to flinch. He gestured to help me up, but I refused his hand and stood up on my own. My mind was strangely quiet, and I was confused about what to do as I waited for him to make the next move. He made it clear that I had lost, and he was in control. As I straightened my clothes, I saw him in my peripheral vision, working the revolver and unloading the remaining bullets into his hand.

"You passed," he said, glancing up at me as my jaw went slack.

"Sorry, bro, everyone gotta get tested." At this, he snickered and handed the revolver to me. He may have won earlier, but I was about to take that shit back. Feeling the need for redemption, I overcame my desire to get the fuck out of there. Instead, I took the gun from him like it was any other regular purchase. This is how fucked up I became in an instant. Overriding the most powerful biological mechanism a human body could produce and powering through it as if nothing happened, I shook it off and went about trying to buy the gun he'd just pressed to my head. Steadying myself as I looked it over, I grinned and waved it around like I had done with the rifle. I defaulted to Ricky, looked at the man who'd almost killed me, and asked, "This thing straight?" This was street terminology meaning had the weapon been stolen or used in another crime. I held the revolver in my hand, tracing the serial number that appeared to be scratched off with the pad of my finger. "Hell, no," the man began. "Got it in a burglary."

This meant the street value of the weapon was much lower, so I offered $100. The man guffawed, causing his arms to flail, revealing various bruises and track marks on his fragile skin.

"Shit, this is a $300 gun, all day," he said, not knowing I knew only cops pay full price.

"Best I can do is $150 as it sits," I stated.

"Naw, you're crazy," the man said, standing firm.

"Well, if you'll sell it at $150, get ahold of me," I replied, handing him the revolver back and watching as he loaded it back up.

As the words poured out of my mouth, I glanced up at the door, which, at that point, looked foreign. I'd gone from thinking I'd never leave that hotel room to wondering why the fuck so much time had passed—and why my SWAT team wasn't blowing the door off its hinges.

I was exhausted and—quite frankly—out of fucks. I cut the conversation short, ripped the comforter off one of the beds to wrap around the rifle I bought, then told the informant we needed to leave. We exited without another word to the assholes in the room, which seemed okay as they were speechless too. Joey walked us down to my van and took the blanket back after I loaded the rifle in my back seat. Before he walked away, he apologized for his friends' behavior, telling me that guy was always like that.

"I'll call you when I get some extra vests and guns, man," he said.

The informant and I slid into my van in dead silence. I thrust my keys into the ignition, feeling relief at the engine's rumble, and took solace in the familiar stench of my van. I wheeled out of the lot, not thinking about what just happened. My only thought was to formulate a plan to arrest the room full of tweakers. Having been saved by my informant, my ego was broken, so I could only muster one stupid question.

"You good?" I asked her.

"Fuck, Ricky," she sighed. "Why aren't you freaking the fuck out? This kind of shit ever happen to you before?"

"Maybe," I responded simply, even though this was the wildest shit that had ever happened.

"Well, fuck," she exhaled, looking weary. "You know they were packin' that room up while you were down, right? His girlfriend told us he was so spun out that she knew he was going to kill you."

"Nah, I had that," I told her.

To acknowledge that she had saved my life meant I would also have to acknowledge that I had lost control. To do that, even briefly for the sake of that conversation with her, meant accepting that what I had done was not just dangerous but also reckless. And that recklessness was a result of my ego—an ego that believed I could control and manipulate anything and anyone to meet my goals, whatever they may be. Looking back now, I realize I was so caught up in regaining and retaining that sense of confidence and control that it didn't even cross my mind to thank her for not letting me die in a repulsive motel bathroom.

It was in my best interest to tightly pack up the emotional reality of the incident and shove it to the back of my mind. As long as I buried it down and made it unrecognizable, the reality that I was spinning out of control would remain hidden. What had just transpired had scared the hell out of my informant, and she had already experienced a lifetime of horror. When I dropped her off, I felt a sinking feeling. She was going back to her practically inescapable life on the streets, and I was headed back to the office to embark on hours of paperwork that would quite possibly out her as working for the police. I wrestled with the decision to let these fuckers go for now to cover her.

I got on my radio and told everyone to keep watch and not move. They were all confused. As far as they knew, the buy had gone smoothly, and they were ready to head home. I called a meeting in a vacant lot and described what happened. Against my wishes, the tactical supervisor working that night demanded that I write a search warrant and have our SWAT team arrest everyone in the motel room that night. This may as well have put my informant on a billboard as a snitch for every criminal to see.

Not long after the informant and I had made it out of the area, the asshole who had put the gun to my head left with his girlfriend for a nearby gas station. Officers stopped and arrested them, seizing several thousand dollars, a quarter pound of meth, and two handguns. One of those handguns was the revolver with a scratched-off serial number that had been found tucked away in the man's pants.

An hour after having the gun violently pressed against my head, I was back in my office, typing up a search warrant for the motel room. I would get advice from our administrative detective to be as vague as possible—just talk about the guns and meth being present and barely mention my assault. This would limit the information that would be publicly available and, hopefully, shield my informant. As I proofread the warrant, details about the surveillance of the hotel room flowed out of my police radio. To my surprise, the man hadn't lied. The revolver had been stolen in a burglary. Time seemed to slow as I read the title of the report: it was labeled a homicide. The homeowner had interrupted a burglary at his home and was subsequently murdered while trying to defend himself. This gun was one of several that were stolen from the man's home following his murder. My eyes glossed over with tears at the realization that I was almost the next victim.

We almost died today, I thought.

The moment the warrant was signed, my SWAT team rushed to the motel room in full gear, ending Joey's stay at the Super 8.

Joey was arrested for selling me a stolen gun along with methamphetamine. I came to find out the wild-eyed, shirtless guy in the bulletproof vest was a federal fugitive, and he was arrested on his federal warrant. The younger girl was a juvenile runaway; she was taken home to her aunt's house with no charges.

I need a fucking drink, I thought to myself.

Then, my phone pinged.

A dealer from earlier in the day was just now getting back to me and had finally resupplied. Never giving up on a buy, I bothered my partner to help me one more time and made the buy just before making my way home. I just couldn't stop myself.

In my garage at 3 a.m., I stripped myself of my second identity, then stepped over the threshold of my house. Determined to build a wall between work and home, I made the intentional decision not to let Ricky into the house. I instituted a rule that I had to take my clothes off in the garage and leave them there until it was time to don my "work uniform" again.

I ambled into the guest bathroom, took a quick shower, and then made my way to my three-year-old daughter, Brenley's, bedroom. As she lay there, with perfect rosy cheeks, long eyelashes, and tiny fingernails, I kissed her forehead and rubbed her back as she slept. I then quietly entered my and Wesley's bedroom, walked to my pregnant wife's bedside, and pressed my lips against her face. That was as close as I let Wesley get that night. I told myself that it was because I never wanted to have her worry about me. But, realistically, just like any other addict hiding my vice, I didn't want to be put in the position of answering to someone who wanted me to stop.

Just as an alcoholic needs their next drink, I needed this work. By keeping the truth from her, I was hiding my "bottles," so she wouldn't make me quit and take my drug away from me.

I moved through the house quietly, then settled on the couch in the living room, in my underwear, staring into the abyss.

When you completely and utterly fail in this line of work, a million thoughts run through your head about all the ways you could have done "it" better—whatever "it" may be. Of course, 99.5 percent of those ideas are entirely unrealistic—stuff you'd see in the movies and fantasize about making a reality. Maybe I could have single-handedly disarmed a crazed man with a gun who had me cornered in a motel bathtub and fought off his tweaker sidekick. Oh, how much mental gymnastics I ran in my head to protect the belief that if I had just done *this* and *that*, or *that* and *this*, of course, I could have regained control. It had been hammered into us at the academy: if you just worked hard enough, stayed sharp enough, knew all the things, watched all the videos, and learned from other people's mistakes and critical incidents, then you would, of course, be able to keep yourself alive. And, come to think of it, they have to *make* you believe that. If I didn't think I could win every time, I couldn't do this job. There is a degree of blind arrogance that is required for those who run into dangerous situations so frequently.

As I sat there that night, staring into the darkness of my own living room, I had another first of my career. *Maybe I can't do this job,* I thought. *I froze for the first time ever. Maybe I can't act under pressure.* This was the same thing that would get new recruits belittled on patrol. I had done this to them myself hundreds of times. But now I was the one who couldn't perform, and my ego took the hit.

Right behind that thought came a roaring train of shame. *My informant never should have needed to save me. I'm such a pussy.*

A repulsive wave of disgust came over me. I felt sick knowing that I had slipped up and compromised my life; I'd gotten us into an unpredictable situation, and I was pissed about it. I was mad at myself for not dominating that room and missing some of the signals I'd been given. Until now, I'd always come up with an answer and made the right decision. The hardest part was that I couldn't find the right move in hindsight either. I found out later—many years later, when it was too late—that what had changed that day was that I'd lost the ability to check my gut and read my own fear signals.

I couldn't recognize that my competitive self-image was vying for more attention than my safety and intuition.

After overcoming my initial shame, I began assigning blame for everything that happened in that room. I later learned that blame is what someone does when they are so intolerably uncomfortable that they can no longer stand it, so they push discomfort out onto others. I blamed my SWAT team for not saving me and my partner for not hearing what was happening. I carried my shame and blame silently, never saying a word about it, holding that anger in for another day or the next target.

After going through something like what I had just experienced, you might think that I'd spent days, weeks, and maybe even months feeling different. Oddly enough, for me, only the following day felt strange—and that was it. An hour into the workday, everyone had moved on. The next day, I would too. A few people checked in with me, and in their minds, I assume it was probably genuine. But, as this subculture tends to do, those check-ins almost immediately turned into them telling their own war stories about a time when "blah blah blah . . ." It's clear now, but it wasn't then. This was what you had to do when you were in this line of work: bury the fear by telling a story with a wild and crazy punchline.

You may be thinking, "Hey, I'm sure an incident like this led to someone in charge giving a lecture on 'lessons learned.'" That absolutely did not happen. In fact, no supervisor ever said a word to me about it, let alone try to get a read on my mental status after something like that. What did they do? They got on my ass for how much overtime I'd burned. I was seething with anger over the total lack of acknowledgment of what had gone down. But the longer I sat in it, the more I rationalized it, and I eventually decided it was better that they didn't say anything at all.

If you let this job affect you, it means you're not cut out for it, I told myself. Then, I locked the residual horror away inside, determined to assume my role.

A normal person would have experienced that night at the Super 8 and either requested a new role, moved units, or at the very least taken a break from UC work. A person in their right mind, with a healthy respect for risk-taking, would have experienced this and undergone a major ego correction after nearly dying. Not me. For whatever reason, I doubled down for several more years. Instead of being humbled and developing a healthy respect for my own fear, I became committed to racking up as many "W's" on my card as possible. But just winning wouldn't feel good enough—I had to do it at the greatest risk level to get the biggest adrenaline hit.

That night was a pivotal one—the night Ricky fully took over. It was the jolt that tipped me over and marked the moment I lost who I truly was. I completely erased any sense of danger or fear from my life. It had no place but to get in my way, as I had just experienced. Being afraid made me lose control of my buy and of my suspects. I would not allow that to ever happen again. I decided that fear had made me freeze, and I felt ashamed of the fact that my informant had needed to save me. The lesson I learned? Bury any bad incident, as it will cause hesitation. Get rid of fear, and you'll perform better. Now that Ricky had taken over, I was no longer just playing a role at work. He was with me, always.

CHAPTER 6
BACKPACK

Throughout my career, I had over a hundred informants. Some were as normal as anyone in my family, working with me in exchange for leniency on a felony charge they'd caught. Addiction can grip anyone and drive them do things completely against their true self. However, most informants were on the opposite side of the spectrum and were not the type of people I would ever choose to associate with. Working with my squad was always voluntary on their part, and the reasons they chose to help us varied from the aforementioned prosecution leniency to the simple greed of easy money. There were also some who were drawn to it for the "cool" factor, as if *they* were the ones undercover. No matter the motive, their personality quirks always earned them a nickname that would become their undercover name.

One of the craziest informants was a man we called Backpack (who got that nickname because he stole them so often). Backpack was a giant headache nobody wanted to work with

—at first. He was a homeless Navy veteran who'd served in the eighties, but never during wartime. Then, one day, someone introduced Backpack to crack cocaine and *Bam!* It blew his fucking mind. One crazy high got him addicted enough to flush his entire life down the toilet.

Suffice it to say, his use of crack made him an unstable soldier and led to him being kicked out of the Navy. He dragged his ass back to Kansas City where he lived with his mom until she—understandably—kicked him out. Since the nineties, he'd been a shithead we all recognized and loathed, with a record of breaking into businesses, stealing bikes, and showering in the McDonald's bathroom sink, causing countless hours of wasted manpower every year.

I knew Backpack from my days on patrol. He'd always be in the area where I worked, stealing bikes from the hipsters who loved hanging out in the art district. We'd arrested him at least two hundred times, but the only consequence Backpack ever faced was going clean for a few days. There was no rock bottom for him—jail just gave him a better place to stay.

Over time, Backpack set up a system where he'd get fast cash in the Westport entertainment district by hustling white guys with a dope man. Backpack and his network of several dozen dealers had an arrangement: the more customers he could bring in, the bigger finder's fee he'd get. Though he didn't deal directly, he connected the people who wanted drugs through a dealer.

Backpack's willingness to act as a middleman for a nominal fee made us confident that he could be bought. A few patrol officers I knew had a connection with him and talked to him in hopes he'd start working for my squad as an informant. They began showing him leniency, trying to preemptively stop him from breaking the law. I eventually met with him undercover and told him we'd keep officers from bothering him—as long as he wasn't on a stolen bike or caught with crack on him—provided he promised his loyalty to us. It then became my job to find a way to get his record cleared so we could maximize his impact on society. So, I negotiated with the court system to make it happen, and Backpack had the fucking audacity to be nervous about it.

"I just don't know if I can work with the cops, man," he said.

"Listen," I began. "I'm getting you a free phone. Do dealers give you free phones? No. You're gonna make money doing all the shit you normally do, except instead of ten bucks or a crack rock, I'm gonna shell out fifty for every buy. I don't know what there is to negotiate here."

He looked at me leerily, then said, "Fuck it. I'll give it a shot."

To this, I scoffed and said, "Let's roll with it for one day. If you hate working for us, I've got other things I've got to do, and you can go back to stealing bikes, being someone's bitch, and getting cuffed for it."

Backpack was a hell of a ride from the jump. One hour in, he proceeded to do the most unnecessary shit, like try and take a bike right in front of me. Habits are hard for anyone to break, and informants always had a hard time remembering that even though I looked like them, I was still the police.

Our first assignment involved trying to do a buy at Alcazar apartments in the Westport area. The place was on the gentrified side of town among neat little shops, boutiques, and dive bars, but hadn't yet been renovated. Hell, it was in such bad shape that the best option would have been to tear it down. The roof was faded and slumping, there were old bars on every window and door, and the stench from inside could be smelled from the street. We rolled into the complex through the back door to meet up with one of the known dealers inside, of which there were dozens. The hallway covered in layers of paint that failed to cover the greasy fingerprints all over them. The ominous, stretching corridor smelled like cigarettes and rotten feet. We plowed through to room 104—Backpack knew the route like the place was his second home.

Once inside the apartment, I bought six crack rocks, then left the complex to fuck around for a bit out on the streets. Backpack decided to invite me back to his "honeycomb hideout" since it was nearby. It was a weird little hut in a downtown thicket, walled off by bamboo that was somehow growing in the fucking heart of Kansas City. In the middle was a rancid, rain-soaked futon covered in gin bottles.

"What the fuck, Backpack?" I asked him. "Why would you rather live here than get clean and live with your mom?" He would just laugh at this and give a careless shrug.

"She don't want me around . . . says I'm worthless. But she lets me come home once a month to wash my clothes!" he exclaimed, as the most jovial, childlike smile spread across his face.

"Well, goddamn! Can't beat that!" I responded, chuckling with him, unsure how or why the dude was just so fucking likable.

Backpack and I would end our day on a sour note—one

that was my fault. He made a call to a dealer and let him know he had a fresh white guy to spend money. These dealers loved the idea of taking a white guy's money. When the man showed up, he caught me in a relaxed mood, which led to me making a mistake. I handed the dealer my money and put my hand out for the crack, just to have him speed off, almost taking my arm with him. Dude took me for $40. I knew better than to let my money walk. Backpack apologized profusely then reiterated that I should never let go of my money before I had my dope.

Several days later, I was walking in Westport with Backpack after just finishing a crack buy in a Walgreens parking lot. A gold Landcruiser pulled up, and all I heard was, "Hey, Uncle, get your white boy to spend with me!" I looked over and it was the same fucker who had stolen my money a few days prior.

I fired back, "Go fuck yourself, you took my money the other day, bitch." This started an argument, which I took seriously, like I was getting even for the previous slight. The dealer did not appreciate my disrespect and jumped out of his truck and ran straight at me like a bull.

Without hesitation, Backpack jumped in front of him and took him in a big bear hug with his long, gangly arms.

"White boy got a gun, man, don't do it."

I did have a gun, and Backpack also knew I had a full SWAT team a few blocks away that would come crashing in the moment the fight started. Backpack stepped up like a big brother and ran the dealer off, even though it meant no free crack from him again.

That was the beginning of a beautiful friendship.

Soon, Backpack wasn't the only one with a nickname. When we were on the job together, he affectionately referred to me as his "white boy." I like to think I was a good influence on him, too, because he never stole another bike again. He did continue to steal backpacks, but we worked on that.

He wasn't the brightest, but for all the times he left me dumbfounded and outraged, I found myself laughing my fucking ass off at his antics. After working together with my partner-in-crime for a couple of months, I could no longer stand watching him return to his shithole hut or bathe in fountains. So, I occasionally rented him a hotel room to get him off the streets and, eventually, we helped him sign up for a veteran's program to live in an apartment rent-free.

Backpack made a bigger difference in society than most law-abiding citizens. He was responsible for several hundred firearms being taken off the street and the capture of a dozen murderers, and he helped us dismantle several large-scale heroin and crack empires. As a bonus for a great job on one case, we gave him a thousand dollars in cash and begged him to use discretion on how he spent it.

In truth, I should have known better. Backpack was the type to lose anything not tied down and somehow always weaseled his way out of the clutches of consequence. This time, though, his poor choices would lead to something more devastating. The night he got that envelope of cash, he went out and hired two ladies to party with, then purchased enough crack for the group to stay high all night. His heart couldn't take all the screwing and drugs, and he ended up having a heart attack in his newly acquired apartment.

Backpack died on his 62nd birthday with the assistance of

the money we gave him to afford a better life. I never got over the loss of my friend and I was heartbroken that I could never tell his mom just how great of a man he truly was. Like my squad and my team, Backpack had become family. Despite his annoying petty crimes, he wasn't a bad guy. In fact, he was one of the most honest men I'd ever met. He was just a guy who struggled with addiction, and, given the nature of my job and my addiction to it, I really couldn't fault him for all the same characteristics I couldn't help but see in myself.

CHAPTER 7
JUNKIE

As Wesley's second pregnancy progressed, I hardly made it to any of her doctor's appointments, feasting instead on a steady diet of dope buys. I'd been on the job for a little over a year and was essentially processing fatherhood through the super-fucked-up lens of a doper. Fatherhood as Brent was one thing, but I'd already survived so many near-death experiences as Ricky; I couldn't stop fighting for his life on a primal level—even if it cost me my true identity.

I made it a priority to keep my family in the dark about just what kind of life I was living away from home. The justification I used was the same false pretense: that I was saving them from worrying about the dangers I faced. They had no clue as I came home smiling, hiding my day's work in the most lawless part of society behind a mask. Even when I missed family events, it was understood that it was just part of my job. I did as much as I could to make life normal for them when mine was anything but.

While my personal life was undergoing a major transition, I found myself immersed in the biggest case of my career up to that point. Until then, I had only bought small amounts of dope. However, one night, while buying a half-ounce of heroin, I found myself being introduced to someone with kilos of it.

During the rare times when Wesley and I actually got to spend quality time together, I preferred to blather about this big case rather than talk about our baby. Always supportive, the only thing she could do was rest her hand on her large, pregnant stomach and say, "Wow, Brent, that's so crazy." However, in her wildest imagination, she could have never conceived just how crazy, as I had intentionally left out the most alarming details.

My early cases were almost all meth and crack, but this case pulled me into the Mexican drug cartel, whose dealers were pushing large amounts of heroin and meth across the country.

One such person was Ted—a local painter and idiot who just really, really loved prostitutes. Ted fell into the cartel by accident, but once he found himself tied to them, he was not allowed to stop.

Ted was ordered to move four kilos of heroin that another dealer had abandoned. The cartel wanted a $50,000 cut but told him he could keep whatever profit he made off of it. One of our informants happened to get pissed that Ted didn't give her enough free heroin, so she introduced me to Ted, which required me to pretend I was a drug runner moving between Kansas City and Chicago. It was a big deal, and it obliged me to be away from my family as it evolved into a wiretap case.

The high point of all of it was that I really got to be Ricky 2.0. Normally, I was Ricky, the half-homeless addict, but for this gig, I got to clean up: I wore skinny jeans, a backward hat, and was clean-shaven. Of course, working with more sophisticated dealers and addicts meant I had to be more strategic in my operations. This inspired a slicker, more conniving side of Ricky that occasionally concerned me. The case was so all-consuming that it wasn't just another thing I could strip off in my garage. I could feel the role I was playing fusing all the more with my true identity.

When my second child, Blake, was born, I took time off work for three weeks—the first time I'd stepped away from running the streets and buying dope since joining the undercover squad. Granted, in the hospital, while my wife was in labor, I would sneak away and go on my fucking phone, working the entire time. To this day, I, Brent Cartwright, am not proud of this, but I wasn't myself then. I'd fully devolved into a junkie. I walked, talked, and dressed like one; I rode continual waves of adrenaline and was always jonesing for more when I was away from my squad, informants, and life on the streets. Though I would never have admitted it, the only place I really wanted to be was in my shitty teal van with a pocket full of crack.

Even though I planned to take all three weeks off for my paternity leave, I constantly texted and fielded calls from work and informants. Within ten days of Blake's birth, I learned about how much slack my team had to pick up in my absence, which made me feel like shit. That afternoon, we decided to compensate for my leave by breaking back onto the scene as a squad, doing a full run together where we hustled around town to buy dope in groups of two and three.

Back in the streets, I felt more at home than I had in my own house, which should have scared me, but it didn't. I reasoned that the thrill of the deal must have been the closest thing to actually doing dope. It was exhilarating, visceral, and hard-hitting. Then, immediately after, came the inevitable comedown and the fact that every deal after was less intoxicating—which gave me something to strive for.

In dope houses, I was the first to bow my neck, get brazen, and negotiate harder. I'd be as slithery as possible, just to see what I could get away with. Somehow, the crack rocks had become as mystifying to me as they were to the motley street informants I ran with. I was not immune to them sucking my soul dry. My eyes shared the darkness of every doper I'd done deals with. I was hungry to manipulate, to threaten, to brawl, and to face death. All the things that had made me an upright public servant and person of character began to dissolve in my brain and bloodstream, as a more sinister evil coursed through my veins.

CHAPTER 8
BUD ICE

I was so fucking good at what I did because I was no longer just playing the part of Ricky. I *was* Ricky, inside and out, working in overdrive 100 percent of the time. Since I was doing buys all day and all over the city, I had to change up my strategies between every buy—demanding a different version of Ricky hundreds of times each month. I'd go from a withdrawing heroin addict hitting up dudes in the hood to buying Percocet pills from nineteen-year-olds in the nicer suburbs. Dressing as a homeless crack addict in the arts district was a completely different vibe from hanging out with the mid-twenties meth group in the middle-class area just north of the city. My ability to come up with storylines and pivot on the spot made me successful at cornering some of the scariest dealers in Kansas City. However, this constant fluctuation led to complete confusion about my true self.

Dope dealers are not overly smart, but they are sharp.

Most never forget a face, especially the features of those working in larger set-ups or peddling drugs over state lines. One confession, misstep, or bust could cost them their lives, so they'd memorize every detail about the cops involved in their incarcerations and seek revenge, sometimes even from prison. In general, they'd assume that a bearded white guy or a woman who wouldn't suck a dick for crack was "the police." So, I really had to get my shit straight, because the odds were against me just for being white. During deals, I knew to keep information straight; I never mixed up the details I'd shared. The department constantly rotated my vehicles out, but I was thoughtful about not repeating my routes. My goal was to never be caught doing the same thing twice.

Maybe the most ironic thing about living a double life as a tweaker was that no sober, innocent passerby would have guessed I was a cop; yet the most incoherent dope fiend would always have an innate suspicion about who I really was, and they'd pick up on any sign of hesitation, nervous eye contact, or exaggerated body language. This could kill any deal I had with them or with anyone they were around.

I often wished we could convert these dealers and addicts into detectives to interrogate suspects because they would, without a doubt, be great at sniffing out liars and fakes, even better than my squad's sharpest investigators.

These people who live a life of total lawlessness have the ability to think on their feet in wildly unpredictable circumstances; they also didn't fear death, as they cared about cash more than they cared about staying alive. They prioritized drugs over everything else. By this point in my career, I was just like them. My own highs took precedence over the risks, and even death. These animalistic survival instincts couldn't be taught in training; I'd been living the part for a long time, and they still didn't come to me 100 percent naturally.

Looking the part got me through the first six months or so, and I passed the test with any small-time dipshit dealer. But even though I'd put so much effort into my looks, they were not entirely necessary. Many addicts didn't look like Backpack, Kenny, or even Ricky. There were so many successful businessmen and women who scoured the most dangerous parts of our cities for the hardest of drugs. They were not immune to doing the worst things imaginable in order to get high.

When I first "put on" Ricky, I really believed I could shed him at the end of the day. This was easier when I was just taking off my disguise of dirty clothes and leaving them in the garage. I discovered that being successful in the field was easier if I committed to being a liar and a fake *all* the time, not just while I was on the clock. The more I loosened my grip on my values and moral compass, the more impact it had on my psyche, but I wasn't open to acknowledging the change, especially not with my loved ones. Without even knowing it was happening, I morphed into Ricky until Brent was totally forgotten. Though the Brent part of me would have once shuddered to watch me overwrite my core values of integrity, dignity, and honesty, the Ricky part only cared about winning on the streets.

There was only one way to do undercover work successfully long-term: surrender to the process entirely and let my alternate personas take over. Once the remnants of Brent were scrubbed away, it meant less of a chance of getting caught and exposing my team. All I saw was that the job became easier and my worries about being caught off guard by a bad guy were now gone. I mean, they couldn't call me out for being "the police" if I wasn't really a cop anymore.

Over time, Ricky's dominant characteristics—grandiosity, greed, and recklessness—were rewarded with continuous dopamine rushes. I could ride the high of "getting away with" a crime, outrunning cops, and escaping death with zero repercussions on my personal life. One part of Brent that never fell away was my creative mind and sense of humor, which had me constantly toeing the line (or leaping over it). The reason these never left me was because these qualities helped Ricky succeed.

One of my longest standing partners was a short, athletic woman with long, straight hair named Dani, who I never saw wearing anything except pajamas or nurse scrubs and flip flops. She always had a serious look on her face, even when she laughed, that made everyone she made eye contact with wary that she would stab them with scissors. We joined forces any time Ricky needed a sister or girlfriend to go with him on buys, and she was subjected to my crazy humor and out-of-the-box thinking more than anyone.

One night, I pitched the idea of incorporating a hooker into our night. Our squad did this occasionally because—as a general rule—prostitutes knew more about drug dealers than they did about their own fingers and toes. If they had money in their pocket, they could make a phone call and have dope in-hand in a matter of minutes.

We would usually just offer girls a ride and buy them some food. If we let them control the conversation, they would quickly bring up sex and we would (obviously) decline. After gaining goodwill and not trying to stick our dicks in them, it was pretty easy to have them call up some dope and make a quick buy. But on this night, I felt like putting a different spin on things.

My particular plan for the buy would involve me inviting a "lady of the night" to hook up with me and my teammate—a request no prostitute would ever anticipate receiving from a cop—then essentially saying, "Hey, instead of sucking my dick, let's all go get high together." The idea behind suggesting sex between three people versus Dani and I paying individually for "favors" was that there wasn't enough room for a group to do the act comfortably in my van, as the front seat was littered with trash, and the back contained about 900 pounds of scrap metal. This meant we would have to go back to the home of the woman we picked up. Ideally, if we made it to her place, we could identify her pimp (who we anticipated to also be her dealer, as there was a lot of overlap), then arrest him in hopes of liberating her from his grip. We planned to navigate the situation by only bringing enough money for crack and not the threesome. Once we were presented with the option between sex and crack, we'd score some rocks, then say we were short on cash and needed to split. Dani rarely argued with my ideas but never celebrated my plans. So, we fleshed out how we could best play the part of two crackheads in love who were looking for a good time.

At that point in my career, I had changed up my *Gritty Ricky* look for a few reasons: a series of busts had gone down where I'd been identified on the streets as a cop. There was a swarm of tweakers who'd done enough deals with Ricky that there was little chance I could throw them off without doing an overhaul. Plus, I still had to take my kid to school in the mornings, and I had frankly gotten kind of scary-looking—I was sporting some pretty gnarly dreadlocks and had given up on trying to clean the grime from beneath my nails and the inside of my ears. I'd definitely received my fair share of judgmental looks from all the other kindergarten parents. Beyond that, I was just fucking sick of the mop—it was always in my face and smelled sour most of the time. So, I ditched Long-Haired Ricky for Mullet Ricky and even added some fade lines to my sideburns to give the cut extra flair.

On this particular winter night, my mullet was matted from having worn a beanie all day. This got a laugh out of Dani, who wore stained sweatpants, a white tank top, a silver bomber jacket, and her hair in a messy bun. Together, we puffed on cigarettes, scouring Independence Avenue in my dingy Ford Windstar, where many of the street prostitutes hung out.

It didn't take long for us to find one such lady. Kisses was a young girl in her early twenties who looked like she was in her mid-forties. She stood on the street corner in skinny jeans and a stained, pink puffer jacket, and was all too eager to get out of the biting winter cold and climb into the back door of my van. Once inside, it became obvious that she was completely out of her element. Dani and I began our usual barrage of conversation: the more we overshared, the less we looked like cops. Kisses met our yammering with silence, which I broke with a pretty blunt suggestion.

"Let's all get high and make some bad decisions together," I said awkwardly. My offer fell flat. I glanced at Kisses in the rearview mirror; she appeared to be turned off by what I'd said, so, I decided to take the weirdness and run with it, proceeding to make another joke in an attempt to loosen her up.

"C'mon, how 'bout a little sandwich action?" I asked. "Ya know, you're a piece of white bread, my girl's a piece of white bread, and I'll be your meat." Kisses uncomfortably shifted in her seat. It was evident she was used to leading the conversations to weed out the cops who did prostitution busts.

"My girl and I live pretty far out, and we want to get this shit going," I continued. "Let's do this at your place."

With no hesitation, Kisses said, "You can come home with me, but I need to call my man first to find out how much to charge for a three-way."

I nodded, never suspecting Kisses was running a scheme all her own.

As I drove to the apartment three blocks away, Kisses proceeded to whisper in Dani's ear; I hadn't really noticed it until Dani locked eyes with me in the rearview mirror, indicating I should pay more attention. Once we reached the dilapidated complex, we followed Kisses out of the van through a run-down courtyard and up two flights of graffiti-covered, half-rotted wooden steps. We then reached the top balcony, and Kisses shoved her key, which shared a keyring with a mini pepper spray can and a jumbo, pink rabbit foot, into the doorknob. She pushed the door open, and we followed her into her pitiful excuse of a living space: a tiny one-bedroom with green shag carpet, wood paneled walls, mismatched lawn chairs, dumpy furniture finds, and a tiny television. In front of the TV sat two of Kisses' neighbors, as it was the only place to watch shows in the complex.

She kicked the couple out and began pressing numbers on her flip phone. As soon as someone was on the line, she lifted her phone up to her ear and disappeared into the next room. In her absence, Dani told me what Kisses had been plotting in the van.

"She wants you to leave," Dani whispered. "She said her man was much better than you . . . that your fucking ugly mullet is proof of it. She said she's 'willing to share.'"

Well, that was a kick to the balls.

So, I did what anyone in my position would do: I raided Kisses' refrigerator. A mostly full 12-pack of Bud Ice was sitting there for the taking, so Dani and I each cracked a bottle and started swigging. With Kisses still missing, we began looking around her apartment.

Down the hallway was a bedroom with a mattress on the floor, surrounded by piles of lacy bras, knee-high boots, and sparkly miniskirts. On the bed lay a four-foot-tall Chuckie doll, sitting as though he was watching over the room. After Dani and I finished our drinks, we returned to the kitchen for another round, where Kisses joined us after her phone call.

"Hey, little mama, you want a beer?" I asked.

"No," she shook her head, waving a crack pipe in my direction.

"C'mon," she nodded, "Let's go back to my room." Dani and I followed her lead.

Once back in Kisses' bedroom, she told us that her man would be back in a bit and suggested we get high in the meantime.

"We'll figure out the cost of the three-way once he gets here," she said, committed to the ruse that group sex was happening. I knew she still had every intention of nudging me out of the situation, I just wondered how she'd go about doing it. Kisses then lit her crack pipe and began smoking; she closed her eyes for one long inhale, then handed it over to me so I could take a drag. I grabbed the pipe as she stood to her feet and started traipsing across the room, picking up odds and ends from the floor.

I lifted the crack pipe as though I was going to smoke but stalled until Kisses' back was turned. Once she was distracted, I threw the pipe under her bed, then stood and joined her in picking up her clothing—focusing specifically on the bras, of course. Once again attempting to get a laugh out of Kisses, I clasped on a sheer purple bra over the top of my shirt and jacket and flounced across the room while chugging and finishing my second beer. My partner followed my lead by grabbing and sliding on a pair of turquoise shimmering knee-high boots; she then strutted over to me, extended her hand, and twirled me around. I pulled Dani into my arms, lowered her into a slow dip, then thrust her back up onto her feet; she pranced on her tiptoes, then shimmied to the bed, where she grabbed Chuckie from the stack of pillows and started dancing with him.

We'd really gotten the party started when I caught a glimpse of Kisses, looking a little uncomfortable now that we'd taken over her bedroom. My partner finished her beer shortly after I did; we were both fully dressed in Kisses' clothes and made our way into the kitchen for another beer.

Dani led the way back into Kisses' room as I eyed the clock on the wall, wondering when her pimp would show. The second we rounded the corner, Kisses asked me where I'd put her crack pipe.

"I gave it back to you," I lied. She sat, nose crinkled, scratching her furrowed brow with her fake red fingernails. The longer she sat in confusion, the more priceless her expression became. She then started rifling through her belongings, eventually locating the pipe under her bed. She took a long hit, then passed it to Dani.

In an attempt to give Dani time to ditch the pipe, I demanded Kisses' attention by jumping up, stepping across the room, and reaching for a curly blond wig at the bottom of her open closet. I asked Kisses to "style me"—gesturing for her to join me in front of the mirror, admiring the purple bra I was still wearing and a pair of underwear covered in sequin stars that I'd stretched around my hips. In the mirror, I watched Dani covertly creep toward Kisses' clothes hamper, then drop the pipe into a pile of laundry where it would likely never be found again. After a few moments, Dani and I returned to our seats on the bed, where I removed the matted dome of fake hair, then placed it on Chucky's head.

Bzzz. Bzzz. Bzzz.

The vibrations came from my back pocket.

Dani slipped her hand inside the pocket of her jacket.

The buzzing continued for a few more rounds as we grabbed our devices nervously.

Our boss.

He was parked outside and super pissed about how long we were taking.

If he finds out I've been in here crossdressing and drinking Bud Ice, everyone's gonna be fucking pissed, I thought.

I attempted to detract any of Kisses' suspicions by nonchalantly heading to the kitchen for another beer. I rounded the corner to find a large figure standing in the doorway. There he was—Kisses' boyfriend, the pimp. I then did what any welcomed guest would do: I slinked around him, barely acknowledging his presence, grabbed two beers out of the fridge, then headed back to Kisses' room. I rounded the corner swiftly, arm outstretched to hand the beer to Dani, when the pimp rushed up behind me, grabbed my other arm, and yanked me back through the doorway and down the hallway toward the kitchen.

"I want to have a talk with you," he said, gesturing for me to take a seat at a sagging card table. He broke the news to me that group sex wouldn't be happening; I half listened while also pricking my ears up to Kisses talking to Dani in the other room.

"Let's kick him out," she pressed. "You've gotta get to know my man!"

This again? The nerve!

The pimp then began to question me. He asked me where I was from and where I was staying. I deflected his questions by asking my own—each regarding the price of different "activities" I could enjoy with Kisses. He showed no signs of anger, so I kept the questions going.

The stalemate finally ended when the pimp reached into his jacket pocket and pulled out several tiny bags of crack, rationed into ten-dollar portions.

"You really should just buy your shit and leave," he insisted, implying I should leave without Dani—which wasn't happening.

I took sixty dollars from my pocket, then reached for six tiny baggies full of crack on the table.

"I wanna buy the rest of what you've got, but I really don't have that much cash on me," I said.

"It doesn't have to be cash," the pimp responded. "You get any android phones?"

"Yeah," I answered, "I can break into some cars and try to steal some shit."

"I'll trade you one crack rock for each phone," he offered.

"Deal," I said.

With that, I stood up and headed to Kisses' room.

"Baby," I called to my partner. "We need to go right now." She didn't hesitate to round the corner and meet me in the hallway. At this, the pimp became visibly irritated.

"Just leave her with us until you come back with the phones," he directed. By that point, Dani and I were making our way to the doorway as though we hadn't heard him. He then reached for my partner's arm, missing only by an inch or so.

"I need her with me," I said. "We have a system."

With that, Dani and I walked out of the door and back

down to the Windstar. Purchasing crack from someone inside the apartment would satisfy the search warrant requirements at the time. There would be no need to go back into the apartment and risk the pimp getting violent over losing a new girl —or getting us back once he realized we'd drunk all his beer. We slid into my car and drove away, never to return again.

CHAPTER 9
JESUS, TAKE THE METH

At times, there's a progression in the dope world where a user sees the money and dope available and aspires to become a dealer. The problem is that tweakers cannot control their own consumption of the product, so they'll use their stash to stay high for days on end. This leads to using up most of their supply, then desperately seeking options to recoup the money they recklessly injected or smoked. This inevitably results in robberies that serve to feed their immediate need and help them regain their supply. Then, the cycle repeats itself, and the risks these kinds of people are willing to take become even greater.

Stealing from family and friends is usually the jumping-off point; even though, eventually, they'll be forbidden from coming around, which leads to property crimes and street robberies. The most desperate will even attempt to rob their suppliers—which was the position I found Carl in when we first met.

Carl was an all-state wrestler from Missouri. He'd been on a steady decline through seven years of heavy drug use. He'd use any drugs he could get his hands on, but meth was his preferred poison. After several years of smoking, Carl started sustaining highs that kept him awake for up to five days at a time. His visceral lows and withdrawals were gruesome, and he'd often endure them on the floor of a jail cell after getting himself incarcerated. Determining he'd had enough experience with the product, Carl delusionally decided he would try his hand at dealing meth. The problem was that he fucking loved it—so much so that he'd spend his first week on the job smoking his supply instead of selling it.

Banned from his family's home after countless thefts, Carl found himself rifling through the suburbs, bouncing between random houses each night, frantically lifting thousands of dollars' worth of stuff to make up for a month of flying high. My first deal with Carl would end up being my last because, out of all the crazy shitheads I'd scored from as an undercover cop, Carl was one of the most unstable.

I called up Carl based on information given to me by an informant. I knew getting robbed was a major likelihood. I had to put my ass on the line; I couldn't ignore the case and let the man keep spiraling, knowing he'd, at some point, end up making some very damning decisions that would cost him or someone else their life. But my ego saw this as a challenge —something I was always up for.

My initial conversation with Carl was short but informative. His enthusiasm oozed through the phone. The guy was jonesing bad for money. He asked me at least four times how much cash I had on me, even though it'd become pretty clear that he didn't have any meth on hand. That could only mean he was suffering from withdrawal. Desperation had fully set in. He needed bread or meth—and he needed it now.

After we'd agreed to meet up, Carl changed our meeting place at least five times. This was a huge red flag that something sinister could happen, so it put all of us on high alert.

I had yet another new boss, Sergeant Coppinger, or Frank, as we named him. He was not thrilled with the way the deal was shaping up. He was on the fence about me doing the buy, but he knew there was no telling Ricky jack shit. I, perhaps too confidently, reminded him who I was and assured him that I had everything under control.

I'll be the one who does what others would back away from, I thought, completely driven by my ego. I had no idea my arrogance was leading me to do something incredibly fucking dumb. But the adrenaline had kicked in by that point and I knew backing away would plunge me into a pit of depression. If I didn't get my daily dopamine hit from the run, I'd face a withdrawal not so different than the one Carl was experiencing.

We're probably both as sick as one another . . .

On some deep level, I was certain it was true.

"Ricky—no tripping with this dude. If he wants you to take him somewhere, call that shit off immediately," Frank urged.

No fucking shot, I thought, while nodding my head *yes* to indicate I understood. I laughed at the thought of calling off a buy; that wasn't something Ricky had ever done, and he wouldn't start today.

"I'm a block away," I told Carl over the phone, feeling as calm as if I were driving to pick up my kid from gymnastics class. But I had a distinct sense that this wasn't going to go down like a normal buy, and I got off on the excitement of that. No, I didn't have a death wish, and I didn't want to be robbed—I just didn't fear either possibility. That's the thing about the streets: once the fear of them diminishes, the true threats that could cost you your life no longer register. I was selectively blind and numb. I'd made too many deals by blatantly disobeying my superiors, at that point. I loved proving everyone wrong: pushing dealers to do insane things, then having great stories to tell about it later, even if (actually, *especially* if) it infuriated my bosses. And this night would be no different.

"I'm here, parked alongside the road near an old mural," I told Carl over the phone. A few minutes later, my eyes landed on a scrawny silhouette staggering toward me through a dumpster-lined alleyway that stretched between two old apartments. Carl's appearance under the orange streetlights was jarring: he had dark, sunken under-eyes, greasy, short hair, and pinpoint pupils that stared right through me.

No way this crazy fuck is coherent.

I sat there, scratching my balls, darting my eyes back and forth—this was just me being me; it was no longer an act. I knew there was no chance Carl could make any logical decisions, but this didn't scare me because he was a skeleton. If a fight were to break out between us, I could snap him in half. I stared him down with confidence, sure I was totally in control of the situation.

Carl tugged on the door handle of the rickety Taurus I'd gotten the keys to that afternoon. I reached over to manually unlock the door and watched him jump in the vehicle, teeming with the same elation I'd heard over the phone.

"We need to drive to get our shit," he told me.

Paying no regard to Frank's instructions, I immediately obeyed.

I drove slowly, making sure I was easy to follow for the surveillance team. My listening device, planted in the console cup holder, allowed my partner to hear every fucked-up thing Carl had to say. He was already amped up—twitching and writhing in the front seat and hanging his head out the window, panting like a dog as we drove. Every few seconds, his long, skeletal fingers would reach for the stereo and he'd max out the volume—blasting the Kendrick Lamar CD that was playing. I found myself becoming more irritated as we drove, knowing my listening device couldn't pick up a damn thing with all this noise.

He reached for the knob once more when I'd finally had enough.

"Keep your dick beaters off my stereo, man," I spat, reaching forward to turn the music all the way off.

This didn't deter him from hitting the *on* button and singing along to the second verse. Then, he stopped.

"How much money you got?" he asked.

"I told you, motherfucker. Get my dope and then you get paid," I replied.

"Bet, I just wanted to count it out!" he said, chuckling.

I knew Carl had no meth, so I couldn't figure out what his plan was—if he even had one.

Then, surprise, sur-fucking-prise, Carl gave me a big explanation about how we actually needed to go to his supplier. Once there, he planned to pick up an ounce of meth. Of course, he asked me to give him the cash first. To that, I raised my eyebrows and chuckled. *Not a chance in hell.*

We drove through each block slowly, and Carl continued to badger me about the cash. I knew his type too well: the minute I gave that little tweaker any money, he'd jump out of the moving vehicle and take off running. It was exactly what I would do if I were a desperate meth head. Carl reached for the volume knob and turned it all the way down as a grin spread across his face.

"Hey, man, my dude will never expect this shit. I'm gonna take his shit when we get there!" he exclaimed, sticking his bony pointer finger in the air as he spoke, as if he were relaying the greatest fucking idea in the world.

"Dude, don't be a dumbass. If you're gonna do it, do it when you're not riding with me."

I could sense his courage growing quickly.

"Nah, man, I'm going to surprise him with this!" he exclaimed, then began digging in his waistband. I knew what it was before I even looked over. I glanced in his direction to see a gleaming black handgun in his palms.

"I'll just get in there and be like . . ."

As he spoke, he lifted the gun, forced his arm in my direction, and pointed it at my head. I'd been held at gunpoint a handful of times and felt nothing but anger as I locked my eyes on the road, feeling my jaw tense as Carl yelled, "You're gonna give me all your shit, motherfucker!"

I white-knuckled the steering wheel, now really fucking pissed off—but not scared.

Carl cackled.

We sat in silence before Carl's voice rang through the car again. "Like that!" he concluded. "That's how I'm gonna do it."

Still driving with one hand, I reached up and, in one swift motion, I broke the barrel over his hand and disarmed Carl. While lowering the gun into my lap, I shot him a stern look.

"Don't you ever point a gun at me again, motherfucker," I said. Then, I did the most ludicrous thing I could have possibly done: I handed the tweaker back his weapon.

At this, Carl laughed. "Man, I'd hate to accidentally shoot you! Like that scene in *Pulp Fiction*! Don't worry, though, that wouldn't happen anyway—the shit's not loaded," he assured me, sitting up a little straighter as he had the evident epiphany that he needed to load his gun.

He then racked the slide and put a round in the chamber.

This made me lose my nerve.

"Dude! I need you to knock it the fuck off! You ain't robbing anyone if you're rolling with me," I told him.

And just like that, Carl couldn't help himself. He started waving the weapon around again, excitedly repeating his plans—this time in greater detail.

"I'm going to walk into the dude's house and tell him to bring his shit out," Carl stated. "Once he comes back with his stash, I'm going to shove the gun in his face—like this!" As he finished his statement, he raised the gun up to my head a second time.

Before the barrel touched my skin, I snatched the weapon from his grip.

This time, with an even more commanding tone, I looked at Carl and said, "If you point this gun at me one more time, I'm going to fucking shoot you, dude."

My threat brought Carl's excitement down. He nodded at my demand, then asked for his gun back.

"You ain't gonna rob your dude, right?" I asked him. "We have plenty of money between the two of us."

"So . . . are you chipping in on this then?" Carl asked again.

This time, he had worn me down.

"Fine, motherfucker," I answered.

We parked one block away from the supplier's house. Carl had stressed that the guy would freak out if we pulled up in his driveway. Knowing this was common among dealers, I agreed to park out of sight. Before he got out of the car, Carl tucked the gun back into his waistband, then pulled out a small roll of cash. Reluctantly, I added two hundred dollars to the cash pile.

"I'll be back in less than ten minutes," Carl said, then walked quickly toward his supplier's house.

The moment he was out of sight, I got a call from my surveillance crew. "Ricky, did you say stop pointing a gun at your head?"

"Yeah," I answered. "I think I talked him out of the robbery, though," I said with a small chuckle.

"Ricky, we are not letting this guy get back in your car," the SWAT supervisor barked. "Once he gets close, we're going to arrest him."

"Got it," I responded, frustration evident in my tone. I felt as if my team didn't trust that I could handle this situation.

True to his word, Carl came walking out of the home about ten minutes later. He was practically levitating with an idiotic smile on his face. It was obvious he had the meth on him—everything about his body language showed he was excited to get high very soon.

Once Carl rounded the corner and was out of his supplier's sight, an undercover SWAT car pulled up alongside him. Of course, he was experiencing such a rush from purchasing a new supply of meth that he had tunnel vision. He didn't even flinch when a group of officers jumped out of a slowing vehicle and then began rushing toward him. Only when they were five feet away from him, guns drawn, did he realize what was happening.

Carl reached for the gun in his pants and the meth in his pocket that he'd just purchased. He then threw the bag of dope straight up in the air, as though he was making some kind of deal with the meth gods to save him. He also released the gun, which soared upward but failed to disappear into some ethereal cloud, as I'm sure he'd hoped. The weapon almost hit him directly in the face when it came tumbling down. He didn't even try to run; he placed his hands behind his back, allowing the team to arrest him on the spot.

"I don't know why you're doing this to me," Carl said. "What did I do?" he added, staring directly at his bag of drugs, which had landed on the open concrete a few feet away from where he was standing.

What a fucking trip, I thought, letting out an exhausted chuckle at the whole ordeal—until Frank's voice came over the radio again.

"We need to talk, Ricky," he said, his voice grave.

I knew that tone. He was fucking pissed, and I would be getting a lecture. The only thing I would have to offer—which, quite frankly, gassed me up—was that I had remained in control throughout the whole buy, and everything had worked out.

I met with Frank in a run-down parking lot, where he warned me to knock this shit off and start listening to him unless I wanted to get killed. All I did was remind him that I had more experience than anyone and I knew what the fuck I was doing.

I didn't want to end up dead, but I also knew that nothing would change.

I was one of the best at this job, and I needed him to let me do my own shit and quit trying to fuck it up.

I replayed the conversation in my head while sitting in the car, sighing as I realized that nothing I could say would change his mind.

Instead of taking my usual route home, I headed to the local community center. It was League Night—a chance to crush my buddies at volleyball. As I passed through the center's sliding doors, I scanned the room for the huddle of familiar faces, all outfitted in similar sweatshirts and shoes. "What up, peeps!" I called out, waving with the arm that wasn't holding my duffel bag.

A cheer erupted from the group, and one of them cupped his hands around his mouth to bellow my name: "RICKY!"

"Wayno!" I said, clapping him on the back. Wayne and I were high school buddies who still got along great. Our wives had instantly clicked when they met and remained best friends. "How you doing, buddy?"

"You know, same old bullshit," he said with a grin. "What crazy story do you have today?"

"Oh, man." I chuckled. "You'll never believe what happened today."

I leaned against a nearby wall and told the group what had happened—everything from the drug deal to the potential robbery to having a gun pressed against my head—laughing off the day's events. Like most first responders, I told the story as if it were a scene in a movie and not real life. As if there were no actual consequences for what I'd done.

They laughed with me, settling into the story as if they heard one like it every day. I sprinkled in causal phrases like, "I mean, can you believe that asshole did that?" and "He really thought that was going to make me flinch," not showing the slightest hint of fear. They probably figured it wouldn't be right for them to freak out because *I* wasn't freaking out. And I did this all the time, right?

My brain was so skewed that I couldn't even recognize my experience as negative. Spouses and family members of any first responders see the same in their loved ones who come home and flatly report seeing a burned body or decapitated baby. As we tell these stories, we forget that they're real and fail to attach proper human emotions to them. This separation, in the right amount, allows us to handle this intense job day after day. However, the underlying trauma must be addressed at some point.

Wayne laughed as loud as the rest of the guys. "That's so crazy, dude!" he said, shaking his head. Years later, I discovered that despite seeming unaffected by my stories, he'd expressed his concern to his wife. Of course, he knew he wasn't allowed to tell Wesley any of what I'd told him, and his wife was sworn to secrecy. But my perspective shifted entirely when he repeated, "That is so crazy, dude," and his grin had faded to a worried frown.

CHAPTER 10
726 BLACKWOOD DRIVE

The one thing I loved most about working undercover was the way the squad shared a ridiculous sense of humor, trading pranks to keep shit fun. My lack of self-regulation proved to be a problem, however, causing me to behave and act in ways that were totally out of line—not just on the job, but off duty as well.

Frank was still my boss, unfortunately for him. I learned that he and his wife were going out of town for a vacation and assumed their kids would be staying at his parents' house, as they usually did when he traveled. I'd searched Facebook Marketplace for a hideous work of art with a plan to hang it over his bed as a "welcome home" present. I was stoked when I found the perfect piece: an oversized painting of a large, fluffy white cat. It was hideous and the size of an 85-inch television. *This is going to be fucking priceless,* I thought to myself. So, I set the plan in motion.

Frank was a big dude—he was massive and country-strong. We had a running joke that he was going to take my ass out back and beat me up if I didn't stop doing stupid shit at work. Given my role as strung-out Ricky, I was pretty thin during this time, so there was zero doubt that he could whoop my ass. Somehow, this fact didn't deter me; instead, it made the idea of fucking with him even more exciting.

My online interactions with the guy selling the painting seemed fine to me. But when my partner RJ and I went over to pick it up, he noticed some warning signs that I'd been oblivious to. Apparently, I had become too accustomed to weirdos.

We rang the doorbell, and the seller cracked open the door an inch. He appeared to be wearing a purple jogging suit and had a pretty vile square mustache.

"Oh, there's two of you?" he began, his mouth twisting into a frown. "I only *need* one of you."

What the fuck? I wondered, glancing at my partner.

"I'll take the little guy," the seller said gruffly. Clearly, he meant me.

"Yeah, I don't think so. We're both coming in," I asserted.

We stepped into the house, and only RJ had the feeling that we'd end up in this guy's basement. The man directed us to follow him down the hallway, where we noticed the house was completely empty—no furniture or appliances anywhere to be seen. Wires protruded from the walls like a spider's web and that was it. Once we reached the master bedroom, I was surprised to see he just had a mattress on the floor, covered with one sheet and no additional bedding. There, the cat painting was propped up against the back wall. I then paid the guy in cash and—luckily—exited with the painting as easily as I'd entered. Only after leaving did RJ open my eyes to the guy's creepiness—that dude definitely had a plan to rape me.

At around 2 a.m., I drove to Frank's house and broke in through the garage door. I tried to carry the giant picture, tools, and screws in one trip, but dropped my drill on the kitchen floor on my way to the living room. As I tried to juggle the massive picture frame and pick up the fallen gear, I heard the voices of his mother-in-law and three small children resounding from upstairs. When the upstairs hall light switched on, it hit me. Holy shit, someone is home!

I grabbed hold of my fallen drill and waddled back the way I'd come. I raced out the garage door, leaving it open as I ran down the block laughing, until I reached the spot where I had stashed my van. I tossed everything into the back and sped from the neighborhood with my lights off, having surely scared the shit out of everyone in the house. I never looked at anything I did that night as wrong. It was an acceptable prank—I'd just miscalculated. Yet, it easily could have ended with me being shot.

Self-regulation is the ability to control one's behavior, emotions, and impulses. I'd lost that. Committing a felony for the sake of a prank was something Brent would never do. But at this point in my life, it seemed funny as hell.

Losing my ability to regulate my impulses and behavior was on full display in my work, too. When Frank got word of what happened and realized I had stopped by, he threatened to take me out back and beat my ass for real. That was until I showed him the masterpiece I'd purchased for his home. He cackled when he saw the big fluffy cat painting, and we hung it on the wall at the office to give the piece the attention it deserved. Looking back now, I can see I wasn't the only one who had lost my self-awareness.

Another prank I played on Frank was taking his truck keys and hiding them. I placed them inside his desk but left a riddle behind for him to solve that would reveal where they were. It was no ordinary riddle, though. I'd intended the ordeal to be more of a scavenger hunt.

Oh no, I lost my keys. Where could they be? Better check the handicap latrine . . . the first note read.

So close, but my mistake. To find them go to where you'd cook a steak . . .

After the fifteenth note, Frank realized there was no end to this quest, and he made it clear that he'd had enough.

"That's fucking it, Ricky," he said. "You're on your bike for your buys," he said. I could tell by his intonation that he actually meant it.

Normally, I would have had zero problems with this, except it was summer and over 100 degrees outside. My bike was BMX-style, meaning it only had one gear and no working brakes. I'd ridden it to a few deals before, but always found myself winded and walking it to locations that sat on an incline. I could tell he was pretty fucking livid, so I didn't fight the punishment. I chose to see it as just another pivot.

I planned to ride around on the bike, get sweaty as hell, and be glad that it only helped my persona. For effect, I packed a backpack full of dirty clothes and added some costume enamel paint on my teeth that would stain my gumline a really nice yellowy-brown. Then, I set out to do some buys.

For some reason, not being behind the wheel of a car—even a busted-up, piece-of-shit car—made my buys easier. It seemed like it made dealers more relaxed; they asked fewer questions because nothing about this mode of transportation said, "police."

Prior to this night, I had completed a few buys at 726 Blackwood Drive, located at the far east end of Kansas City. The place was in terrible shape, and the city was planning to tear it down within the year. The fact that it was still standing created a problem for the street it was built on—it attracted thieves, addicts, and prostitutes, turning the area into an absolute cesspool.

I had purchased meth from several dealers who stayed at this house, and I had obtained a search warrant for the home. I chose this day to serve the order. My goal was to do what was best for the neighborhood: to use my case to have the house boarded up and fast-track its demolition. This would make the dealers scatter, and some of them hard to find—at least for a while—but the kids in the area would finally be able to play safely in their front yards, and parents of the block would feel some relief.

Prior to serving the warrant, I stashed my bike behind a bush and met up with our SWAT team to run through the details and verify the suspects involved in what was about to go down. We piled into one of their vans and drove past the home to confirm that the correct house would be the target of their enforcement.

The place was so run-down that it was hard to look at. Trash was piled outside, windows were busted out, and an odor that smelled like death reached all the way out to the curb. This was common for meth houses. They were the most disgusting spaces known to police: common breeding grounds for fleas, rats, and roaches—usually amongst piles of dirty clothes, rotted food, and heaps of destroyed electronics. It would be unfathomably dirty, and my SWAT team would get the honor of meticulously searching it for drugs. To be clear, they hated me for this.

Once we'd talked through the buy, I informed the team that I was going to approach the house on bike one last time and attempt a confirmation buy. My goal was to ensure there was meth on hand and that a few of our suspects were on the premises. If they were, I would have more weight behind my request to have the house torn down. After the buy was complete, I'd signal the SWAT team to come in and execute the search warrant. The team agreed to this idea, then I returned to my bike and peddled up to the house.

I usually found meth buys moderately fun but never thrilling. The only thing that made them interesting was that I could approach the scene from any angle I wanted. Sometimes, I'd get stupid with it. There were plenty of opportunities to add humor to the set-up and make the work fun. Infusing hilarity into potentially dangerous scenarios made me feel like I could handle hair-raising tasks with less hesitation. When I could drape something sinister in dark humor, the dangers of the job were often forgotten.

Once I'd hopped on my bike, I made a kind of a jackass move. I intentionally sped off too quickly down a hill—knowing full well I didn't have brakes. I jumped the curb a few times just to dick around, attempting my best trick rider impression. I neared an intersection and really wanted to put a smile on the surveillance team's faces, so I ran my bike straight into a thick patch of bushes. Wondering who would be the first to mention my skinned-up elbow, I broke into a smile.

By the time I made it to the front walk of the dope house, I was sweating through my shirt. There was a broken gate out front, connected to a chain-link fence overgrown by weeds and ivy. The weeds created a little thicket on the inside of the fence where I hoped to hide my bike, knowing it was highly likely that it would get stolen. Normally, a front yard with a fence would have prompted me to look for a guard dog, but I reasoned that the grass was way too high for me to worry about that. These small yards were patches of solid dirt, usually caked in mud if there were dogs around.

I approached the front door without a single worry, still laughing at myself for the crash in the bushes, smiling ear-to-ear to show off my enamel-painted teeth. The door was then opened by one of our main suspects: a 6'6" black man who towered over my 5'10" lanky ass.

"What the fuck do you want?" the guy questioned.

In my early days on the job, I rehearsed every line ad nauseam and was nervous as fuck. Now, with experience, I just smiled and made shit up on the spot. I held up my arm, which was gushing blood from the fall. My elbow and wrist were smeared in damp red streaks.

"Sup, man, can I get a Band-Aid?" I asked.

"You're at the wrong house," the suspect stated, then

stepped outside, squared up to my chest, and tried to intimidate me off the porch.

"I'm just playin'. Mickey here?" I asked. Mickey was our other suspect at the house.

This made him step back and curiously ask why I wanted to talk to his friend.

"He just knows what's up," I stated, then I let him know that I had forty dollars to spend.

"Cool," the guy finally said. "Follow me."

The large man guided me three blocks away from the house. We carried on a strangely easy conversation, intermittently chuckling like long-lost friends along the way. We finally did the proper introduction, and he told me his name was Chris. Though I'd inquired about where we were going a few times, he wouldn't answer my questions. My experience taught me this was either because he was out of meth or intending to rob me. Soon, we cut through a thicket of green in an alleyway between houses—out of sight of any prying eyes.

Now completely alone in an isolated location with Chris, alarm bells started to go off in my head, but no fear accompanied them. I began considering which direction I would run if he pulled out a gun to rob me. Ideally, I could escape to somewhere that had people around. Fortunately, though, he didn't rob me by force; he simply *asked* for my forty dollars.

Knowing I was letting the money walk away, I handed the cash over to Chris. He then instructed me to wait there because his supplier wouldn't want a stranger in his house, then assured me he would "be right back." Given that dealers really *didn't* want outsiders in their homes, I couldn't tell if he was lying or if I should really wait.

I then watched Chris cut through three yards between the houses before disappearing out of sight. After a few minutes, I was sure he was gone for good—that he'd gone to buy meth with my money and was off somewhere getting high. Instead of staying in place, I finally made the decision to go wait for Chris at his house.

He's gotta come home eventually, I assured myself.

Once I was back on the stoop of Chris's home, I didn't even bother to knock; I just decided to walk inside like I owned the place. I cracked the door open and began coughing because of the stench, then stepped inside to see trash piled high, along with mountains of stolen cell phones, laptops, and various gaming systems.

Suddenly, a gaunt woman with stringy hair who looked to be in her early thirties, wearing an oversized jersey and way-too-short jean shorts walked out of the kitchen. She asked me where Chris was.

"That's what I want to know!" I fired back. "I'm gonna wait right here until he comes back."

"No," the woman stated. "You need to go outside and wait on the porch."

Defiantly, I pushed past her into the living room, took off my backpack, and flopped down onto the filthy plaid couch with a thud.

"My boyfriend isn't gonna be happy that you're in here," the woman said, placing her hand on her hip.

"Well then," I began. "Why don't you call his ass up and

tell him to hurry the fuck up and get back here? He has my money."

This pissed the woman off. She stood in front of me, her voice getting louder with every word, arguing with me.

I looked at her and smiled.

"You're not making me go anywhere," I stated. "Your shithead boyfriend owes me forty bucks or a bag of dope!"

"Are you a fucking idiot?" she asked. "The first rule of the streets is that you don't give your money to people you don't trust." Her statement was true—but it still struck a nerve.

I stood up from the couch, visibly pissed off.

"I'm not leaving until your boyfriend is back."

What happened next was purely instinctual—not the instinct of Brent but of Ricky.

I grabbed my backpack and moved to a small table near the front window. The surface of the table was covered by a mound of digital cameras, cell phones, and laptops. I figured the items were likely stolen or traded for drugs. From the looks of them, they probably didn't work. I examined the pile, then began stuffing my backpack with the best things I could pick out. The woman was now fuming. She rushed over to me, sticking her finger in my face and screaming loud enough for the neighbors to hear.

"DON'T FUCKING TOUCH OUR SHIT!" she bellowed. "CHRIS IS GOING TO FUCKING KILL YOU!"

I smirked at her, saying nothing, and continued shoving things in my bag. My tactic worked. The woman frantically grabbed her phone and called Chris; when he didn't answer, she left a short voicemail urging him to "GET. HOME. NOW."

Once she hung up the phone, I came to the realization that my little reunion with Chris might not actually end well for me. I carefully started to unpack all of the electronics from my bag and left them in a more organized state than I'd found them. I then posted up near the front door, eyeing the street through the side window. I was not leaving without my meth or my money—I was adamant.

"You're gonna get fucking killed if you stay here," the woman said. Her threat made me do a visual sweep of the room, eyeing the space for any objects she could potentially stab me with. I then impatiently shifted my attention back to the empty street.

Ten minutes later, I saw Chris walking with Mickey a few doors down. They were approaching the house. I didn't let on what I was seeing, said nothing to the lady, exited the house, and immediately approached the two of them as they neared the entrance of the chain-link gate. I wanted to create some distance between the guys and the woman inside. I really didn't need her telling either of them about how I was pilfering through his table of electronics.

"C'mon, let's go inside the house," Chris stated.

His saying this made me realize he wanted to smoke my meth with me to get a free high. At this moment, the girlfriend cracked open the front door and began screaming at Chris. He headed up the front path to the house, my meth still tucked away somewhere on his person.

Not feeling like getting my ass kicked, I called after Chris, hoping he would turn around.

"Hey, man! I want my shit. I have people waiting on me. I gotta get out of here!"

He turned on his heels, immediately suspicious, and began asking me who I was. Mickey shut down the questions, telling Chris that he knew me, and that I was cool. Chris looked me up and down, then reached into his pants pocket to reveal a cigarette pack that held a small bag of meth. Whether it was forty dollars' worth or not, I couldn't tell, but I wasn't about to question him.

As bad timing would have it, the woman couldn't take it anymore. She dashed out of the house screaming, "THAT MOTHERFUCKER WAS TRYING TO STEAL YOUR SHIT!" She was so flustered that I wondered if *she* would try to fight me.

Chris turned to the woman and asked her to tell him what happened. The woman then pointed at me and reiterated, "THAT MOTHERFUCKER TRIED TO TAKE YOUR SHIT."

He hadn't even had a chance to tuck the cigarette pack away before I snatched it from his hands. I'm not sure what came over me—other than the fact that it was purely a Ricky move.

I dashed back to my bike, grabbed it with both hands, then threw it over the fence. I frantically stuffed the meth into my pocket before hoisting myself up onto the metal rungs and leaping down to the road on the other side. I was fully prepared to run away and leave my bike behind. I glanced back at the house, where Chris didn't even appear to be running after me. I reached for my handlebars, stood the bike upright, got a running start, straddled the seat, and pedaled away.

I passed two houses before I glanced back to see he had

attempted to chase me but stood bent over and winded in the middle of the street.

"SUCKS TO SUCK, BITCH!" I screamed, soaking up the delicious adrenaline bump that helped me escape when my life depended on it.

I sped four blocks away to where Frank was staged with his truck, intending to stash my bike and get a ride. I urged him to have the SWAT team execute the search warrant immediately, warning him that Chris was incredibly pissed.

Frank informed me that the surveillance detectives had already called the SWAT team in because Chris was taking his anger out on Mickey. They were forced to go in early to stop the violent encounter between the two of them. Both men were arrested for narcotics sales, meaning they'd be interviewed the next morning.

Given that my squad was a fully undercover unit, we never conducted our own interviews. We deferred situations like these to our dedicated branch of administrative detectives, who would conduct these tasks on our behalf.

Less than twenty-four hours later, when the detective interviewed Chris, he made the surprising comment that he was grateful the police showed up when they did. He explained how some meth addict had come to his house and was attempting to steal his electronics.

"Pussy got away on a bike. I was going to kill that skinny kid," he rasped.

I've always been sure that if I stuck around that day, I would have been seriously hurt by that dude. There was a definite moment of knowing I needed to leave for my own safety—but I would have done *anything* for the deal. I wasn't in control of the situation, but I'd become so used to high-adrenaline scenarios that no one could have convinced me of that fact.

My motto had become, *I have this handled—let me prove it to you.* I was hard-headed. Namely, because my career as an undercover had been full of close calls that always worked out. The feeling of "knowing what I was doing," even when I didn't, pervaded my consciousness. This should have become all the more concerning as time passed because I continued to be a wildcard during operations, never backing down. I refused to give up on a buy—no matter how much danger I put myself in along the way.

One year later, I would find out from another detective that Chris was arrested again. He had ambushed a now-dead man and tied him up in a basement. After a few hours of torturing him, the guy confessed to stealing a ring from Chris and selling it. He lost control of his rage, killed the man, then he and his girlfriend left the body to sit in their basement for a few days before cutting him up and jamming him into a duffel bag so he'd be easier to dispose of.

"I fucking hate thieves," was his explanation to the detectives.

It felt jarring to consider that I could have been the one killed and dismembered by this psychopath. The only difference was that I had a surveillance team to swoop in and save me if shit went south. But that could only help so much—flashing back to the Super 8, this felt like a closer call than I liked. This feeling lasted only a few minutes. Letting these thoughts brew in my head would cause me to hesitate or actually consider death as a possibility while working. And that interference would only cause problems during my buys —or worse, make me realize that I needed a change in my career, thus losing access to my drug.

This was when it should have become abundantly clear that the morals I'd grown up with and lived by throughout most of my life were different from Ricky's. I wasn't intentionally making risky decisions, and I didn't even recognize that I was doing it. My mind was damaged. If Brent had been in that situation or one of the countless others, my actions would have been entirely different. I could have properly diagnosed the danger and made an educated decision that would have deescalated the incident, allowing me to exit much sooner. If I had practiced proper self-maintenance, I would have seen it, but I hadn't, and I didn't.

It was official: I had fully conformed to my work environment. I could no longer see the line between good and evil. And once I lost sight of that line, there was no way of knowing which side of it I was on. The only way to see any line was to stand up and draw it for myself. Of course, having lost my sense of reality and connection to my true self, any line I drew would be incorrectly placed. In addition to this, I had a disastrous chemical cocktail built up in my head, and I had become addicted to stress hormones. When buys were easy, I was disappointed; when they were risky, it was never enough to satiate my hunger.

I feared nothing. My natural instinct should have been to ask important questions like:

Am I making the situation worse for no reason?
Could this get me killed?

None of these concerns crossed my mind anymore. The

same mentality that plagued the addicts Ricky now called his tribe was the mindset that dictated my life. And just like them, I was putting aside my own personal safety to get my high. The thing was, I believed myself to be untouchable—that I could get away with anything and never really get hurt. There was only one outcome that could ever play out: me winning.

I could walk into any buy, confront any dealer or strung-out addict, or take on any case, confident that I was going to be okay.

Soon, this would be the reason I stopped carrying a gun on operations. Because when you're invincible, you don't need a gun. Why bring something into the buy when no one can kill you? Suffice it to say, this was just one of many decisions that would lead to the disastrous end to my undercover career.

CHAPTER 11
LET IT RIDE

I came to expect the unexpected on all of my undercover cases, yet I found myself surprised just about every time I met dealers. This was especially true for those who appeared unassuming or who had evaded detection by the law for decades. Years into my career, I'd learned that if I really wanted to catch the biggest drug lords, an informant was a necessary evil. These dealers didn't rise to the level they did by being stupid; they kept their operations clean and their tracks covered, ensuring they never got sloppy. When these guys fucked up, it was usually after years of "mastering" their process. With a good customer base, they started to pay less attention. That was when they slipped up—by pissing off the wrong person or by outing one of their sellers after they got busted and became an informant.

Once law enforcement had a dealer on their radar, it got easier to start building the evidence necessary to take down their suppliers, who were massive and had made an art of being invisible on the streets. Such was the case with Sean Adams, who would come to be known by the squad as the Walter White of Kansas City. One informant would be the catalyst that brought Ricky into his life and led to one of the more comical stories of my career.

All it took was an expired license plate and a minor traffic ticket to kickstart a federal investigation into one of Kansas City's biggest meth runners. The cops pulled over a light blue Mazda with faded tags and learned the driver had a suspended license and several warrants for her arrest. Once the woman was cuffed, she watched as the officers rifled through her car, then concluded her only option was to negotiate.

"Look," she said. "If they look through that car, they're going to find a quarter pound of meth. I'm delivering for one of the biggest meth dealers in this city. I'll give his name to you guys so long as you keep me out of prison."

Once the tweaker gave our detectives the pusher's name, all were surprised they hadn't heard of him. They called me in on the case, confident that I had at least heard of Sean, if not done a deal with him by that point, but his profile was an absolute mystery to me. Consequently, every guy on the squad called bullshit on the intel, convinced that our new informant was just lying her ass off to save herself from charges.

Apparently, though, the informant told the detectives this dealer was selling at least forty pounds of meth per week. Our records on Sean revealed he'd only had one traffic ticket since the 1980s. If the information was valid, it meant this guy was strategic enough to dodge the police for more than twenty years. It was pretty unheard of, given that, over such a long period, any user was likely to have a knee-jerk response and expose themselves.

When we looked into Sean further, we were even more confused. His house, a modest 1,100-square-foot building with three bedrooms, appeared to have cameras but wasn't heavily surveilled. It was also quiet and rarely had people coming and going. It wasn't until we enlisted one of our financial experts to pull more documentation on him that we learned our informant was probably telling the truth. Sean's records revealed that he'd lost almost half a million dollars at a casino in the first eight months of 2014. His work history suggested he wasn't making nearly enough to lose such a significant amount. Narcotics trafficking was the only reasonable explanation. Once we confirmed that there was some credibility to the informant's statements, the squad elected to send Ricky in—and he was raring to go.

For this case, I was farmed out to the squad that focused solely on meth traffickers. They were one of my favorite groups in our building. I'd built rapport with them by proving I was willing to do anything for the deal. I carried my reckless reputation and their approval like badges of honor. These units and other federal agencies knew they could come to me, confident that I would get the job done. It was a mark of pride to be trusted with a case of this magnitude.

The day after the informant's arrest, I met with her to discuss Sean. Evidently, Sean was suspicious of everyone he knew. He required that his buyers smoke meth before every transaction: a common practice on the streets meant to filter out any police targeting the dealer. He conducted all his sales from his basement and hotels, and it was in Sean's basement that I bought from him for the first time.

The squad determined that my first meeting with Sean should be a quick buy for the sole purpose of establishing our informant's credibility. I would use the informant to get into Sean's house, then try to gain his trust on my own. The informant detailed how she'd commonly score one to three ounces of meth every time she bought from Sean. She also made delivery runs for him, usually hauling at least one pound of meth around the city at a time to make drops for customers.

I figured I'd keep the buy consistent, sticking with one ounce so Sean wouldn't suspect anything unusual with the informant. Unfortunately, I was limited by my command staff on how much I could spend and was forced to ask for a smaller amount of meth than usual. I worried this would throw up a red flag for Sean, and I'd inevitably suffer the consequences because some supervisor didn't want to write a three-sentence memo to pull more money for the buy. In any case, I went with it, hoping that if things went well, I could get more cash for the next deal.

When I picked up the informant for the buy, I was struck by how calm she seemed. Most snitches' nerves were through the roof on their first deal, but this woman seemed fine. Any time I asked her about Sean, she'd talk in circles, and I found myself growing increasingly irritated with her. This left me feeling unprepared and paranoid that she was out to sabotage the buy in some way.

Though I was rarely afraid during buys anymore, I strangely had some reservations about this deal as we rolled into Sean's driveway. Concealing my reluctance, I turned off the ignition, then motioned for the informant to lead the way before we exited the car and strolled into Sean's open garage.

Inside was a man about 5'7" tall, actively polishing a motorcycle. His arms were covered in shitty, blurry tattoos, and his head sagged as if his neck had suffered an injury and never fully recovered. When he raised his eyes to meet mine, they had a sternness that reminded me of facing the school principal as a kid. Without hesitation, the informant walked right up to the guy and opened her arms for a hug.

"Sean, good to see ya!" she said.

Knowing a lot about bikes, I decided this was where I would direct the conversation. Sean's motorcycle was a GSX-R750, identical to one I'd owned in college. Sean and the informant made small talk, leaving me out of their conversation entirely, though Sean kept a cautious eye on my movements as they spoke.

After a few minutes, I cut through the gruff banter. I looked up at Sean and asked if I could ride his bike. He chuckled as if to say, *You can't be serious.* I persisted, though, figuring if I could go out on the busy street and ride a wheelie past the house, I'd pretty much eliminate the idea that I was a cop. I told Sean about the trick I knew I'd still be able to pull off, but he just didn't appear to be into it. His expression was clear: he was never going to let me on that bike, so I should just shut the fuck up.

"Man, we need to pick up some stuff," the informant interjected. "Ricky here's got good money on him." (A term that meant Sean wouldn't have to give out meth on an IOU.) Sean shut down the conversation with a wave of his hand and then cautiously looked around. He then left the garage, glanced over the yard and up the street, then paced back inside, pulled the manual garage door closed, and locked it. Sean walked us inside his house through a small wooden door that led to his kitchen.

"Stay here," he commanded, then walked through the living room and down the hallway toward the back bedrooms. One minute later, Sean lugged a large black bag through the hallway and hesitated near the front door. There, he reached for a two-by-four that was propped up against the wall and slid it over two hooks bolted to either side of the door to create a "dead man" lock. I'd never really been sure where the term for this lock came from, but my imagination led me to believe that if a person needed to save themselves from behind that lock, they were a dead man. At this point, I became nervous. I had been to many drug dens, but never been locked inside in that way. I knew that if I signaled to my squad, it would take some serious time and effort to save me.

Sean walked us to a small door off the kitchen that led down into the basement. Before heading downstairs, he placed a second dead man lock on the door that divided the two spaces. I turned halfway down the creaking, unfinished staircase and glanced toward the kitchen, watching him secure several deadbolts.

As I stepped from the last stair onto the low-pile carpeted floor, a musty, damp stench hit my nose. Sean flipped on the stairway lights, and my eyes scanned piles of boxes and junk stacked everywhere. The walls were built with two-by-fours and wrapped in chicken wire, which created a hallway-like structure that led to a makeshift door made of the same metal. I awkwardly led the way, trying to play it cool while the informant followed me, and Sean walked behind us both. When I neared the homemade door, I eyed a small hangout area with two couches facing six television screens streaming footage from Sean's yard. On the couch, his daughter, in her mid-twenties, sat huddled with her friends. They were dressed cleanly in T-shirts and skinny jeans but had a roughness to their language as they gossiped about who was screwing who.

"Sit next to them," Sean commanded, gesturing for both of them to scoot over. I took a seat on the far left of the couch, where Sean would sit next to me in a red, velvet-lined chair. He then pulled up a small table next to the couch as the informant found a spot on the sofa furthest from us. I glanced around and noticed two men behind one of the makeshift walls, breaking apart different electronics. One man was carefully taking apart what appeared to be a brand-new television, announcing that he was "removing the blue wires from it." He talked at a frantic pace, detailing how he needed to rewire it with a different color because "blue wires are what the police use to spy on people."

The other man had a shaved head that he'd clearly buzzed on his own, as several patches were noticeably missed. He gripped a hatchet with both hands and swung it violently, breaking apart an old boombox stereo to salvage replacement wires. The jarring swings of the hatchet were mere feet from the back of my head, sending adrenaline coursing through my veins as my heart pounded. The group stared until Sean broke the awkward silence by asking what I was looking for.

"I want a half," I said distractedly, trying to act normal while subtly assessing the potential dangers of this strange location. While I waited for Sean to get me the drugs, I talked to the women, slightly hitting on them, but not enough to piss Sean off.

Though most dealers would interpret "a half" as half an ounce, Sean had a different definition. He reached for the black bag from earlier that he'd hauled downstairs and unzipped it to retrieve a plastic tote. Once the lid came off, I was shocked to see about ten pounds of meth inside it. Sean grabbed a scale and a gallon-sized plastic bag, then shoveled a large scoop of meth into the container.

"Dude. I want a half ounce, not a half pound," I told Sean, laughing. He glared at me in disgust, then emptied the bag into his tote. The interaction made me wonder if my informant had misled Sean into believing I had more cash than I did. Sean then stood, reached into a nearby cabinet, and retrieved a butane lighter and a glass meth pipe. He loaded the pipe with a small amount of meth, preparing it without ever taking his eyes off me. I stared right back at him, knowing exactly what was coming next. Sean was going to make me smoke meth to prove that I wasn't the police.

Once the pipe had come out, everyone in the basement gathered in the seating area, lumping together on the couches. They were all getting in line to get a free high, and I was at the front of the line. My mind began racing with ways to get out of smoking, knowing any excuse could lead to questions and more pressure to use. Running out wouldn't work either—the case could be over before it started. It became abundantly clear that the informant had been telling the truth about the level of dealer Sean was. So, I needed to figure out a way to salvage this buy.

Sean handed me the crusty pipe and lighter. The glass bulb had several shards of meth in it and a blackened bottom showing its mileage of use. Any drug user would have fired that bowl up so quickly that they would have burned their face with the lighter. I couldn't afford to hesitate and risk things seeming more suspicious than they already were. I took the lighter in my right hand and the meth pipe in my left.

Sean turned his attention for just a second and began putting the lid back on the tote of meth, and I threw the pipe on the ground, acting as if it slipped and fell onto the carpet. I hoped the carpet would be thin enough for the pipe to shatter, but it didn't. It just bounced over near the feet of one of the women sitting next to me.

Without skipping a beat, I handed the lighter to her, which she was all too happy to have. She picked up the pipe and melted the meth inside, then took a deep breath off the pipe. A large white cloud of smoke plumed from her mouth as she passed the pipe to the next lady. The sour ether-like smell of the meth filled the small area and burned the damp mold smell out of my senses.

The group was so focused on when they'd get their next hit that they didn't even notice I was skipping my turn. The informant helped me out by requesting the pipe before it got close to me. As the pipe was being passed, I turned to Sean to continue making the deal.

"I am coming into money soon . . . from an inheritance," I lied. "All I want is a tester."

Many dealers would provide half an ounce as a test of their drugs, and I was offering to pay for it. I told Sean I needed a reliable supplier to accommodate my needs so that I'd never run out of product. This prompted his ego to take over, leading him to brag that the tote was only a fraction of what he had—that there was a much larger stash in the back and that he could handle any amount I requested.

Once I'd made some progress with Sean, the tote lid came off again, and I pulled out my money. As Sean bagged up slightly more than half an ounce of meth, I gave the informant a nod as if to say, *We have to go*. The informant interrupted the deal, told Sean we had to leave, and initiated our goodbye. I paid Sean and stuffed the meth bag down into my sock, then told him I would be calling him soon. After a quick handshake, the buy was done. The informant and I walked out of the basement and out of the house—our only obstacle being all the damn locks Sean had put in place.

We left Sean's house, and I was flying high about convincing him to open his bag a second time and sell to me. *Management better fucking agree to more money next time*, I thought to myself, knowing a dealer of that level wouldn't keep me as a customer if I weren't continuously spending money. They were reluctant at first, but then agreed.

I would meet with Sean several times over the next six months. Each buy was destined to bring me to his basement. It became so customary for me to descend to the dungeon that I'd go down there automatically while he headed to his bedroom to get the meth.

On one buy, I could hear Sean walking upstairs, so I ran around "the dungeon," taking pictures of his setup for our case. I also wanted to get a better idea of where his hidden cameras were placed. Sean's use of his own product was beginning to lead to mistakes in his actions. Though his work had been immaculate for two decades, he was starting to lose his precision, partly due to intermittent bouts of paranoia, which the informant had mentioned to me.

On this particular day, Sean began yelling at me from the kitchen, infuriated that I'd entered his basement ahead of him —he perceived it as an intrusion. During that same purchase, he told me I'd need to start buying larger quantities or find a new supplier.

"I want you buying multiple pounds, not multiple ounces," he stated, prompting me to convene with the squad to discuss how we could switch up our tactics.

Over the course of weeks, we discovered that a Mexican drug cartel was the source of Sean's meth; this prompted us to progress Sean's case to a "wiretap case," meaning it would require additional regulation, time, and processing from the federal government. The last thing the compliance office asked of our team before allowing the wiretap was to give specific and clear evidence that Sean was still using the same phone number for drug deals. This meant I would need to contact his cell phone to arrange a buy and go through with it before we'd be approved for the tap. Ideally, I'd get the confirmation done as quickly as possible, and the government would give us their shiny seal of approval. The only problem I could foresee was the less-than-ideal timing: it was nearing Christmas, and most of the detectives who should have been on surveillance would be on vacation. This gave me a sense of unease about the whole ordeal.

Nevertheless, I sent a quick text to Sean using our previously discussed code words for ordering meth. We'd created a language: requests for different motorcycle parts specified different weights of meth. For higher-stakes deals, Sean would sell away from his home—usually in casino hotels. There, he'd take a good portion of his earnings and gamble it away, often losing a significant amount of money. Though his losses were piling up, Sean was being offered extended stays in free rooms, courtesy of his accruing rewards points. His response directed me to one of the casino hotels on the outskirts of town, which my team had anticipated.

My cover squad for the operation consisted of two detectives hiding in the stairwell and a sergeant stationed in a parking lot about a quarter mile away. Knowing the hotel room doors were solid steel did little to comfort me; I doubted a rescue would come quickly if we needed one. I asked my supervisor if he'd called our SWAT team for coverage. It was our division's policy to have them listening in, so it only seemed right to ask. He ended up berating me—calling me a "weak little pussy," even though I'd proven I was pretty fucking resilient by that point. It was small jabs like this that reinforced the idea that the more I pushed, the more respect I'd earn. We didn't even inform the SWAT team of what was happening, which was a total no-no.

On the night of the deal, I pulled up in front of Harrah's, the casino hotel where Sean had directed me. I delayed, allowing my two-man wrecking crew to get to the stairwell; I then walked inside. Once in the atrium, I texted Sean to let him know I was headed to the room number he gave me. But first, I went to the bathroom to look myself over, check my listening device, and count my money one last time. I then boarded the elevator and clicked the button to the fourth floor.

Once I reached Sean's room, I used the brass knocker and, finally, the adrenaline kicked in. The door opened to a face I didn't expect at all—a tall, young blonde woman. Given Sean's financial history, I could only assume he'd hired a prostitute. I figured she'd mind her business while we did the deal. She then returned to the bed, where wads of Christmas wrapping paper surrounded her—she was wrapping her kid's fucking Christmas presents while also "servicing" Sean.

Sean greeted me and waved me over to the sitting area, which had large windows that overlooked the parking lot. I sat down on the couch, and he asked me when I'd last seen my informant.

"I haven't," I lied. "I just figured she'd lost her phone."

"Well, it's important you bring her next time," he stated, piquing my curiosity, though I knew better than to question him.

He reprimanded me about working via text message; evidently, he had forbidden the code we'd once used. I could tell he was already high on meth and paranoid; he likely hadn't slept in days. The more he spoke, the more agitated he became. He proceeded to lecture me about how the government had a massive listening device that looked like a big movie reel and was capable of picking up drug talk on every phone in the city in real time. Sean emphasized that my asking to "buy an alternator" meant we were now "both compromised."

Growing more frustrated, Sean started interrogating me, asking questions that I was hellbent on dodging. His voice grew louder as he began to demand names, positive that one of my customers was talking to the police.

"Chill the fuck out, man! No one I sell to knows where I get my shit from!" I exclaimed, chuckling.

"You shut the fuck up and stay right here," Sean commanded before reaching for a bag at his feet containing a lighter, pipe, and a bag of meth. The pressure was on. Sean was determined to get me to smoke. Knowing that the wiretap case was on the line, this presented a huge internal conflict for me. I hated that we'd gone through so many buys, only to watch the case possibly fizzle. I had a decision to make: smoke meth or risk ruining a year's worth of work just days away from finding Sean's supplier. And I had to choose quickly.

Sean passed the loaded pipe and butane lighter so I could take a hit. I could have smoked the meth if I wanted to. There are rules and procedures in place for such occasions in this line of work. But there's no telling what is in any of the dope on the streets. Just as I never want my family experimenting with street drugs for fear of fentanyl poisoning, I didn't want to do it either. Panicking, I intentionally dropped the pipe (the same move I used the first time I was asked to smoke), which enraged Sean. He bent over and picked up the pipe.

"Smoke it right now," he insisted. "I'm not asking." My frenzied, last-ditch effort to get out of the deal came down to the cash in my pocket. I took it out and started handing it to Sean to pay for the meth that I was hoping to get. I splashed the money all over the floor, apologizing profusely as I lit the lighter and started to melt the meth inside the pipe. Sean ignored the cash on the ground, studying me as I boiled the meth. After cooking the crystals just enough to get them smoking, I put my lips on the pipe and inhaled a small amount of the fumes.

The taste was extremely bitter and tart. It stung my tongue and inner cheeks as I held it in my mouth for just a second. As I exhaled the smoke, Sean finally quit watching me and began picking up his money. Pissed off, I tossed the pipe and lighter at Sean aggressively.

I warned him, "If I get spun out and come knocking on your door at 3 a.m., you can't blame me."

"You better never show up unannounced," he stated.

I was infuriated that I'd just been forced to put poison in my mouth. Even though I didn't inhale it into my lungs, I could taste the nasty flavor on my lips and tongue. Sean grabbed his money and tried to smoke the meth, then studied the pipe, confused. He then glared up at me.

"This shit ain't even fully melted," he stated. He fired up the lighter and brought the meth to a raging boil. White smoke now fully coming from the pipe, Sean took a huge hit and exhaled a large cloud of smoke from his mouth. Knowing he was about to pass the pipe, I started to make my exit.

I grabbed one of several baggies of meth from a black bag in front of Sean and headed to the door, rambling loudly as he tried to stop me. I grabbed the door handle, thanked him, and told him I would hit him up later. With a rush in my step,

I walked over the threshold and shut the door immediately. I was then struck with the realization that I'd made a huge mistake.

I'd been in such a rush and was so pissed off that I was looking for any exit. I wasn't paying enough attention to realize I had just "escaped" into the walk-in closet; now, I was trapped inside Sean's hotel room. Thinking quickly, I flung the closet door open.

"See, dude? This is why I didn't want to fucking smoke today!" I theatrically stormed across the room as I said this, pulling open the front door, stepping out, then slamming the door with a thud. I walked quickly down the hall and exited down the stairwell past my support crew, seething but still determined to keep the information from my team.

The last thing I needed was that sergeant making me feel like shit for letting it get that far. I felt like such a failure that I carried what happened inside my mind, letting it fester for months.

Following the hotel deal, Sean started ignoring my texts and phone calls, no matter how much I offered to spend. Because I'd met with him, though, the wiretap would be approved by the government, and we would start to see just how busy Sean was as a dealer.

Sean always seemed to have ten pounds of ice on him. During several of his sales, we would follow his customers away, arrest them, then seize the meth. We were also able to start catching his Mexican suppliers, who transported forty pounds of drugs at a time hidden inside welded compartments in cars. This enforcement action would begin to affect Sean, as he noticed his network slowly getting arrested and his supplies being intercepted. His deals slowed down dramatically, and his losses increased until he pivoted and changed his cell phone number to better cover his tracks.

Around this time, the wiretap needed to be re-established. However, since the government wouldn't approve it on a phone not being used for drugs, we had to get Sean's new number. So, we devised a new plan: Ricky would "accidentally" run into Sean while he was gambling on the casino floor. There, I would flash a bunch of money and play on his greed to lure him back in.

The ATF was assisting in this case, and the lead agent intended to run the briefing before our squad's attempt to do a buy with Sean. Unfortunately, some communication breakdowns began to sow tensions among the team. I tried to put this out of my mind during our briefing and focus on the impending deal. I determined it would be best to bring a partner with me to keep Sean from pushing drugs into my mouth again. Meanwhile, other detectives would be on the gambling floor, keeping a watchful eye on my moves. A few detectives would be in the casino surveillance room watching for Sean to hit the casino floor, marking my cue to bring Ricky out to play.

Sean was known for only playing slot machines in the high-roller area. These slots had a minimum of $10 or more per play. Some also went up to $100 per play. This meant that I would need extra gambling money, just in case it took me a while to get Sean's attention. The ATF gave me $2,000 to spend on meth and $2,000 for gambling. The lead agent warned me against taking money away from a private business while working for the government. His rule was that I couldn't win any money from this casino, and if I were up, I had to lose it.

"Bring me money or bring me meth—and nothing in between," the agent commanded.

On this particular mission, my colleague RJ partnered with me. His undercover persona was similar to Ricky's, but he was new, so he didn't have my confidence. He was goofy and unashamed to do anything weird or crazy, but he hadn't yet learned to work through fear. In scary situations, he would develop a lisp and become jittery, making him look like a paranoid meth head, which, to be honest, wasn't entirely a bad thing. Though RJ once had a bit of an issue with gambling, we weren't using his money, so there was no threat of having anything to lose. I was not a gambler, so I'd need his help if we hit any game besides the slot machines. The first thing we did was hit the bar for a few shots and fresh drinks—then, Ricky and RJ were ready to roll.

I gave some of my gambling money to RJ, so we could both play and wander around the floor. I kept the buy money in a separate pocket as it was all recorded for the case file. When I entered the high-limit area, I saw Sean hiding in a back corner with an older female. They were both at a slot machine, blindly hitting max bet. I set up close enough that Sean could see me but far enough away to make it seem like I didn't notice him. I was going to play hard to get and let him come to me.

Then, in the corner of my eye, I noticed Sean nudging his

female friend and pointing at me. My plan was working. Even better, I hit the jackpot on my second spin that paid out $800. The lights on my machine flashed, alarms blared, and I screamed, "Pay me, bitch!" Sean couldn't help himself after seeing my win. He sent his friend away, then came over to "celebrate."

On the machine next to me, Sean started cramming in $100 bills. I ignored him, forcing him to strike up a conversation with me, "Hey, dude."

"Motherfuckin' boss man! What's up?" I said enthusiastically. "I'm killin' it tonight!" I stepped over, hugged him, and told him how much I missed him. We carried on with small talk, catching up like long-lost friends. I then reached into my pocket and showed Sean that I was on a roll and making big money. I asked if he was still "in business," letting him know that I wanted to spend my money with him. This was enough to get him to take the bait. He told me to meet him in room 105 in one hour, then cashed out on his machine. Though I was thrilled, my celebration was short-lived, as the night was only one-third complete.

Our detectives knew Sean had a large network of associates; they were worried he might have someone watching me on the floor. In order to keep my cover, I would have to keep gambling with the ATF's money. So, I called the lead agent and gave him a rundown of the night. As the conversation ended, I asked him, "What happens if I win a lot of money? Can I buy more meth?"

"Absolutely not," he stated. "Now, cut the shit."

RJ and I went right back to the bar for some more shots, then cruised over to the $25 blackjack table. We'd run our money down in the high-limit area to about $800 each. We sat down and began our play, knowing we needed to kill an hour. After our first few hands, some knucklehead wearing a stupid necklace with giant letters spelling "SLIM" kept taking the dealer's bust card, causing the entire table to lose. After the third time he did this, he was run off the table by all of us angry players. At that moment, everything changed.

RJ and I both hit blackjack on the next hand; then, from that point forward for the next hour we only lost a very small number of hands. The casino then started shuffling out dealers every ten minutes, causing a reshuffle in hopes of slowing our winning. It didn't work.

Four dealers later—we were on a huge winning streak. Knowing that we had money we had to lose, we tipped each dealer as they left. The waitresses came by every few minutes to refresh our beers, gladly accepting our $50 tips each time.

After one hour had passed, I told RJ we needed to take a pause and count our money. We also needed to call the lead agent and ask if everyone was in place for our buy. While discussing the next step, I had to make a confession: RJ and I had turned our $800 into $2500 each—even after buying insane amounts of drinks and tipping like we were loaded. I begged the agent one last time, let us buy Sean out of all his meth with this money. Exhausted by my asking, he responded, "Lose the fucking money and get the fuck out of there."

He was tired of watching us party from the surveillance room. He wanted to go home.

When I relayed the command to RJ, he leaned over and

said, "Man, I can't do that. You can't piss off the gambling gods like this. It's bad luck for life."

"I'll take your money and lose it if that's what you want," I offered. He hung his head and agreed to lose his money alongside me as we ordered one last round of beers, tipping the waitresses $200 each.

RJ and I each put $250 out on a bet and hoped for some crappy cards. We played the exact opposite of what all the blackjack books say to do. We each hit a blackjack right off the bat. I stood up and yelled, "LET IT RIDE!" before chugging my beer.

On the next round, we both had low cards, and the dealer showed a ten. All the books would say to hit, but we didn't draw. Dealer bust.

Holy shit! We were supposed to lose, and we've just made another grand.

Almost as if we were doing it on cue, RJ and I stood up screaming, "LET IT RIDE!"

The waitress hadn't even asked for our order, but she was already at our shoulders, handing us new beers. We took them as fast as she took her next $200 in chips.

All of our shouting brought a crowd to our tiny table. Everyone wanted to see what the action was. The next deal came out with this big stack of chips on the line. Again, playing to lose we made the worst decision possible. And it happened, we lost.

The crowd belted out a huge letdown sigh. *Not my money, not my problem,* I thought to myself.

"Fuck it, let's do it again!" I bellowed.

We then put down another large amount of chips, and RJ

won while I lost. Another chug of the beer and I was cheering and yelling to do it again. With each deal, the crowd marveled at the utterly idiotic bets we made. In less than twenty minutes, this crowd watched us lose our entire stacks, which had peaked at well over $3,000 each. RJ felt defeated, and I was on top of the world, laughing my ass off at the absurdity of it all, drunkenly forgetting we needed to get back to work.

Shutting off the fun wasn't easy, but I helped wind RJ down, and we composed ourselves before heading to room 105 to meet Sean. We'd gotten lost in time, and it'd now been over an hour that we'd kept Sean waiting. I knocked loudly, and no one answered. I knocked again and heard a voice grumble back, "Just a minute!"

Soon, Sean pulled open the door and invited us in. We walked to a small bench couch by the window and sat down.

"Sorry we're late, we just lost our asses on the blackjack table, but we are gonna win it back in a little bit," I said, leaning back on the couch.

Still new to our squad, I could tell RJ was anxious. It didn't help that he had a tic that compelled him to light up a cigarette whenever his nerves got the best of him. The moment he pulled out a Marlboro red and lit the cigarette in the hotel room, a voice coming from Sean's bed yelled, "Put it out, motherfucker! No smoking in the room!"

The woman Sean had been meeting with from the casino floor then sat up in bed, picked up a meth pipe from the nightstand, and lit it. I hesitated, hoping she wouldn't ask me to smoke, and luckily, Sean was distracted with laying out the terms of our deal, so there was no immediate pressure from his end.

I really just needed to make the deal; it didn't matter how much I paid. Still, Sean was trying to rip me off and charge way over the going price, which made my ego flare. *This motherfucker won't get the best of me!* I was adamant. I was still holding a grudge for the bad taste left in my mouth on the last deal. Literally.

We negotiated until the terms of the deal were finalized, and I was now carrying three ounces of meth in my pocket. Sean then handed over his new cell phone number for future deals. I was still engaging Sean in conversation when the woman on the bed yelled at me.

"Get the fuck up on out of here," she began. "You interrupted us, we were trying to screw."

Relief rushed over me as she said this, as it meant I wouldn't have to smoke.

"Happy to leave," I said with a wave.

RJ and I left room 105 and walked down the hotel hallway, riding a high and raving about how crazy and fun the night had been. It was a relief to have a few fun nights as a break from the usual intensity of our work. I put him in a headlock, gave him a noogie, and thanked him for his help. That night, everything seemed to run smoothly; there was no stress of ensuring the deal went through to keep the case from going cold. It was just fun.

As we left the casino floor, RJ was still smoking a cigarette when, suddenly, we heard a loud voice bellow, "Hey, you two, stop! Stop right there!" It had a tone I recognized—one eerily similar to law enforcement.

We had been instructed to operate in complete secrecy; only the security team inside the camera room knew we were here on an operation. No other law enforcement had any clue what we were doing. I looked at RJ and said, "I'm going to run. If Sean has people watching us, we can't cooperate with anyone wearing a badge."

Certain I'd work out the details after fleeing the hotel, I took one last look over my shoulder. That's when I heard the officer continue, "Man, you have to put your cigarette out. You can only smoke on the casino floor."

As he said this, a wave of relief washed over me. There would be no sprinting to the parking lot or bearing the consequences of getting "caught." There would only be reconvening with the agents and detectives to recap the evening.

Out in the parking lot, RJ and I met up with the assisting agent. We told him about our winnings, high-fived over the night's success, and joked about all the free beer we drank. The agent was visibly upset that his part had been far less exciting. He tried to wrap up the night, asking for his money back.

RJ and I looked at each other, confused.

"What money?" I asked.

"The gambling money," the agent answered. "I want my money back."

"You'll need to talk to Harrah's about that," I said. "I can't help you."

"What the fuck do you mean?" he asked. "Don't tell me you two idiots lost two thousand dollars?"

Thinking he was joking, we started laughing.

"*Two thousand*? Shit. We lost way more than that. We lost over six thousand dollars tonight!" RJ exclaimed.

This made the blood drain from the agent's face. It was immediately apparent that he wasn't kidding. I reminded him that I'd called him and he told me specifically to "lose all the money and get the buy done."

The agent was so infuriated that he shook his head, got in his car, and sped away—nearly running over my foot in the process.

Later, we learned he hadn't been clear in his instructions: he wanted us to keep the initial two thousand dollars and only lose what we had won. I would have done just that if we hadn't miscommunicated. Had he not been so hardheaded and opened his stupid ears, he would have understood the questions I'd initially asked.

Once the agent's car was out of sight, RJ looked at me and outstretched his arm with a clenched fist as a shit-eating grin spread across his face.

"LET IT RIDE!" he bellowed, prompting me to ball up my fist before he slammed his knuckles into mine.

"WOOOO!" I howled before doubling over in laughter. "LET. IT. RIDE!"

CHAPTER 12
TACO

My undercover work throughout Kansas City always seemed to come in waves. I got on a hot streak in the nicer southern part of town and spent months down there buying meth. When those months dried up, I found myself back in the newer Northland buying meth and heroin. I could always count on the more violent, lower-income east side to bring in droves of crack and meth. It was clear that meth would always be my specialty, and there was plenty of it in Kansas City.

The east side of KC was known to be the most violent part of town; so, our squad made the area its main target. Modern law enforcement theory has held that targeting the dope slingers in the most crime-riddled neighborhoods will, in turn, lower the rate of violence. In a perfect world, I could pick up a strung-out tweaker whose desperation to get high would drive them to take me, a total stranger, to their dealer. Those drug dealers became my ground zero, from which I would eventually climb the dope ladder and target the main offenders in the narcotics world. Of course, nothing was free, and the usual payment for a "go-between" was a cut of the score. In the streets, for a real user, there are no rules. As much as I transformed, however, I was still a real cop pretending to be a tweaker, bound by the rule of never sharing any dope I bought.

Once you pick up a stranger for the purposes of getting high, they become like an annoying visiting relative who never takes the hint to go home. I became accustomed to kicking my passengers out of my car after handing them an empty, knotted plastic baggie that appeared to contain dope but didn't.

On a cold, rainy day in March 2015, I found myself scouring a busy gas station for someone who had an appearance that screamed, *I get high*. With so much traffic coming and going, it was easy to spot the one guy who seemingly had nowhere to go. His clothes were a mess, his greasy hair looked like it hadn't seen a comb in a week, and he couldn't sit still, like he had ants crawling all over his arms. I struck up a conversation with him and quickly brought up giving him a ride to go get some meth if he took me to get it. Once in my car, I found he was more talk than action; he had neither a phone to call a dealer nor the name of any location that I hadn't heard of before. I could tell he was depending on me, hopeful to leech information on new places he could land some dope.

As we drove, I looked for a good place to ditch him, but suddenly we passed a strange-looking woman he recognized. He began screaming that she had multiple dealers that she could call to get us a hookup. There was no question that something was off with this woman. She had platinum hair that'd been dyed Kool-Aid red; she was gaunt and pale and, as she walked, she carried her cell phone an inch from her face. The dude begged for me to pick her up, emphasizing how many dealers she knew. He fooled me for the ride, but I had no need for him if she was the one with the real connections. I kept going and, in his desperation, he started to open my car door to call out to her—he couldn't find the window controls.

"Stop here, man—she knows everybody!" the guy urged, all while I sped up so I could kick him out a few blocks away and meet up with her by myself.

"I've had enough, fucker; get the fuck out," I said, stalling near a curb five blocks away from where the woman had been. Once he was gone, I turned around and sped back to find the woman. Luckily, she stuck out like a sore thumb—walking, seemingly oblivious, cell phone glued to her face while sipping out of a 44-ounce Styrofoam cup. I slowed my car, rolled down the window, and offered the woman a ride. She opened the door and jumped in like she was never taught the lesson about taking rides from strangers. I knew my previous rider was telling the truth about her knowing several dealers just by how quick and easy she got into my car. A random ride in these streets almost always means we're heading somewhere to get high. She knew this as much as I did, and since I had the wheels, it was all but assumed I would be paying if she provided the dealer.

Once the woman was inside my car, it became abundantly clear why she'd been holding her phone so close to her face:

she had albinism, which caused her to have terrible vision—she was virtually blind. I turned the conversation immediately to dope and, without a pause, she began asking how I wanted to get high, then started pushing me to buy the small bag of weed she had on her. I knew she had access to heavier stuff, so I told her meth was what I wanted.

She used her phone to try to contact some meth dealers. In these instances, I usually tried to sneak a dealer's number off the screen as it was typed in, but she held her damn phone so close to her face it was fucking impossible. Meth dealers are similar to users: they live on tweaker time, and even greed can't speed them up. This always frustrated me, as my true self was always fifteen minutes early. She put her phone down as we waited for a reply and opened her giant foam cup which, to my surprise, was full of cold potato soup. She then pulled a spoon out of her jacket pocket and started slurping it down right there in my car, almost like she forgot about the task of buying meth. As she lost herself in her gelatinous soup, I watched, unfazed. I'd been in so many odd situations that this didn't even cause me to gag. It seemed my body had overridden the sense of disgust.

I was eventually able to swipe her phone from my console, lower it near my thigh on my left side, send several of her contacts to my phone, and then delete the text I'd sent to my number. Habits are hard to break. It didn't even hit me that being sneaky was unnecessary; she couldn't see what the fuck I was doing. I slipped the phone back into place as the slurping continued for several minutes; then, she lowered the cup, looked up, and scanned the parameters of the front seat.

"Where did I . . . ? Did you see where I put my phone?" she asked.

"I think you dropped it down by your feet," I lied.

She scooted her feet around the empty floorboard, then her eyes migrated to the console between us. She reached down for the phone and touched the screen right as she received a text from one of her contacts—Taco.

Taco was a mid-level meth dealer on the east side of the city. This part of the meth world was so intertwined that I had bought from several of his buddies and knew exactly who he was. I just hadn't come across him, until now.

"Hey! You know my dude Taco?" I said, prompting her to clasp her phone more tightly and pull it closer to her body, in an attempt to hide the screen from me.

"He's my boy," I continued, "but I forget the way to his house. It's nearby, right?"

Luckily, this woman was gullible; she bought my story immediately, then called Taco, asking if we could swing by for a deal. Though Taco preferred the woman come alone, he reluctantly agreed to let me tag along after she let him know I was no stranger to him. I sent a text to inform my surveillance crew about where I was headed, then followed my passenger's meandering directions while our additional crew of undercover detectives took their places in the area.

Once on Taco's block, I parked down the street from his address as he had asked. My passenger called him to let him know we had arrived. Once she finished speaking, Taco hung up without a word. Two minutes later, he shuffled down the steps of his porch outside his small, dirt-streaked white house. The few windows and doors he had were covered by solid steel bars.

Outside my car, Taco tugged on the handle of my back door. I pressed the unlock button, which prompted him to swing open the door and then slide into the back seat. He then looked me up and down, confused, as we had clearly never met.

"Where do we know each other from?" he asked.

"Big Mama's house," I answered, without missing a beat. To be a great undercover, being put on the spot like this required an ability to spit out quick and believable bullshit. Big Mama was a very large woman and east side dealer at the heart of the meth world. Everyone in the streets and on the police force knew of her. She took in any tweaker as long as they were valuable to her, and everyone called her Mama.

My lie and pure greed were enough to coax Taco into doing a deal with me. But he insisted we drive around for a few blocks so he could scan the perimeter to see if anyone was following us. After we'd done multiple laps, burning up gas for the sake of meth paranoia, he sold me a small bag of meth, then stashed the money I gave him inside his sock. With the deal done, I dropped Taco back at the same spot where I'd picked him up, and we exchanged numbers before he returned to his house. I then threw a few bucks at the girl for the hookup and asked her where she wanted me to drop her off. She rattled off a nearby address, visibly frustrated, as she'd clearly wanted a cut of the meth. Given that I no longer needed her to gain access to Taco, I disregarded her irritation and let her out close to a nearby meth house.

My intent was to do a few more buys with Taco so I could

get a search warrant on his house. After all, this was where dealers like him would hide their stash of dope and guns. One week later, I called him to get an ounce of meth. Though he'd initially told me to pick him up from his house, he called me at the last minute, asking if I could meet him at Big Mama's.

Fuck, I panicked, having committed to a story with very little knowledge it would come back around on me. I had tried a deal with Big Mama two years prior, but I was a mere rookie to the game then and it did not go well. One thing was made clear during my attempt: she fucking hated me and could sniff out my bullshit from a mile away. She'd made it clear I was never to come around her again. I looked in the mirror at my mangy beard and dreadlocks, figuring my appearance had changed enough since our introduction. When I first met her, I had a horribly crooked mohawk and just a small bit of hair on my chin. She also knew me as Kenny instead of Ricky. So, I reasoned Kenny had been forbidden, but Ricky was headed to Big Mama's house. And besides, I was no longer just Brent pretending to be a tweaker. I had this shit down.

When I relayed my new plan to my boss, Frank, he was understandably nervous.

"Ricky, you know there will be no less than a dozen people inside that shithole, and you've probably bought from half of them recently," he stated.

"And?" I replied.

My assuaging didn't get very far; he insisted I take another undercover detective to come alongside me in case shit got out of control. Luckily, it'd be RJ. If it went anything like our deal with Sean, I knew we'd be in for a good time.

Because RJ was still a little green, I had him carry the listening device and insisted I do all the talking. When we arrived on Big Mama's block, we parked down the street, away from her house, which was surrounded by surveillance cameras.

While walking up to the house, RJ looked at me, grimacing.

"What is it, man?" I asked.

"Dude, I'm sorry," he began, "Can you make this quick? I have to take a shit!"

"Are you fucking kidding me?" I asked, as annoyed as I was amused. "You're gonna have to fucking hold it," I stated flatly. There was no rush; nothing we were doing was so important that we couldn't wait twenty minutes. Hell, it probably would have been more tweaker-legit if we were late. But I was in the zone, and not even my good friend needing a break could stop me.

Knowing that he was about to shit down his legs, I made RJ knock on Big Mama's door just to fuck with him. As he pulled back, I couldn't resist giving him hell.

"Dude! You knock like a fucking cop," I yelled loud enough for anyone inside to hear.

The door swung open, and we were met by Big Mama's daughter. I said nothing and pushed passed her, then motioned for RJ to follow me in as we ignored her blocking our path. Sometimes, you just have to act like you own the damn place.

We walked through the house to the dark, musty kitchen. Dirty dishes covered in crusty leftover food were stacked along the counter. There were several piles stacked a dozen high each, and it looked like no one had washed them in months. We made our way to the living room, and I was shocked to see the scene: an inflatable mattress in the middle of the floor with Big Mama's very large body laid out in the center of it, wearing an oversized muumuu and smoking a cigarette while hooked to an oxygen tank. Fortunately, I didn't recognize anyone but Taco.

Her daughter took a seat on the left side of the mattress, and some guy with a shaved head, holding a machete, sat on the other. At the foot of the bed, in the corner of the room, was a giant bean bag chair that cradled a scrawny guy holding an older woman in his lap while they both played games on their cell phones. At the other foot of the mattress sat Taco, who greeted me with a wave, but didn't stand. So, I did what anyone would do. I found a spot near Mama's mattress and pushed aside any reservations about her outing me as I sat down like I'd been there a dozen times.

I then took one glimpse back at poor RJ, who was shifting on his feet, trying to fight his bodily urge, but nature was calling. He finally interrupted everyone's conversations and asked where the bathroom was. Big Mama lifted her large arm over her head and pointed down the hallway.

"On the right," she said.

I shook my head—RJ was actually going to shit in this unsanitary hellhole. Five minutes later, he waddled in and asked for some toilet paper. Just like I would in the office, I took this opportunity to mock and berate him. Groupthink took over, and RJ unknowingly stepped into the spotlight as the others dissed him with zero empathy.

A roll of toilet paper soared toward RJ from the guy sitting on the beanbag chair. He caught it and headed back to the bathroom as a few more comments hit him on his way out of the room.

On the floor, beside Mama's mattress, I made my deal with Taco and carried on a casual conversation, waiting on RJ to finish. Big Mama never said a word throughout the somewhat awkward business deal. Around that time, RJ returned, holding the toilet paper roll in his hand.

"What do you guys want me to do with this?" he asked. I looked at him, almost pissed off as if to say, *Who the hell brings the roll back out of the bathroom?*

RJ embarrassingly left to put the roll back and it made for the perfect exit. We gave our quick goodbyes to Taco and Mama, then I looked at RJ and waved him to follow me. We walked to the car with ease after another successful deal. For the rest of the night, I laughed at RJ for shitting in that house during a buy.

I would get one more buy from Taco that went much like the first. Afterwards, I returned to my office to write a search warrant for his house. When I researched him further, I found that he had been a suspect in a burglary at a pawn shop a few days prior. During the break-in, Taco had apparently used a homemade bomb to blow up the rear of the pawn shop. He damaged the back door enough to get inside the store and steal multiple firearms before the building was engulfed in flames.

I contacted my ATF counterparts and let them know I was currently buying meth from Taco and was about to write the warrant. They were immediately interested, as the ATF believed Taco had stashed the stolen firearms inside his home. I filed for a federal search warrant for my investigation and got it signed by a judge. Given Taco's long criminal history of violence, the ATF coordinated a large group of detectives within our specialized Gun and Career Criminal Squad to assist with the search warrant. The ATF agent wanted to ensure Taco was home when we executed the warrant, so I would do one last confirmation buy.

Having the ATF assist in the case meant additional conversations and more detailed pre-planning than I was used to. There were actual checklists that revolved around concerns for my safety, which, if I'd had a healthy sense of self-awareness, would have made me realize just how dangerous of a scene I would be walking into. Instead, I reminded everyone of Ricky's track record and essentially convinced them to shut the fuck up about it. I was going and that was that. To my benefit, ATF's involvement meant the use of their fancy equipment while I did my part. I was given a better listening device system so everyone involved could hear me. My usual, shoddy equipment could pick up on some things, but too often left people guessing if I was actually in trouble or not.

I called Taco and asked him for my usual ounce of meth.

He answered groggily, as I'd just woken him from an afternoon nap. Then, he excitedly perked up and said, "Oh, man, get the fuck over here! I got something to show you!" This put everyone on edge, unsure of what to expect. My group's consensus was that it was a setup, but I couldn't see it. I had already fought through the onslaught of everyone not wanting me to do the buy. Going through with this purchase wasn't necessary, as we could conduct surveillance, locate him, arrest him, and execute the search warrant on his home. But a buy was a quicker way to locate him, and I craved the responsibility and the weight of the case resting on my shoulders. Once I'd determined that I was going to do it, there was no stopping me. This was another chance to prove to everyone that I could—and would—do anything.

Once everything was in place, I set out to go see Taco.

This time, I parked in front of Taco's house with a clear view of the solid steel security door. The metal bars on the windows looked even more ominous up close. I knew that if an emergency occurred, it would take officers several minutes to break through the fortified doors. I picked up on every little detail so that when my SWAT team hit the house, they'd know exactly what to expect once they breached the doorway. This was a monumental feat of multitasking. Be Ricky, first and foremost, while memorizing every detail to relay once I got back to my car. Were there dogs in play? Kids? How many people were inside and where were they? What were their moods? Were there any guns? Who had them? Drugs? Traps? What hazards and obstacles were lying around?

I left my car and walked up to Taco's porch, where he stepped out of the front door to meet me. He was shirtless, wearing baggy mesh shorts with a pistol tucked into his waistband. He wanted me to know he was armed. But nothing that should have alarmed me actually did. I knew that he could be luring me inside to fuck me up or even shoot me. Still, I couldn't drum up any fear, even if I tried. I'd lost myself that much while living as Ricky.

We entered the house together, and he instructed me to lock both the deadbolt on the security door and the one on the solid wood front door. With a smile on my face, I pretended to struggle with the locks and just closed both doors. Taco eyed my movements skeptically, then proceeded to secure every lock himself. My plan for a safety net failed.

Once inside, I found myself in his living room, where another shirtless dude sat at a computer desk by the picture window near the door. The living room was small, no bigger than my kid's tiny bedroom, but crowded with the desk and an oversized couch and television. The volume was loud, and it instantly drew my attention to the movie that was playing—*The Fugitive*. The very fucking movie I'd based my undercover name on! As if those odds weren't bad enough, Taco caught me watching the screen and immediately told me that this was his favorite movie of all time.

Not good.

Taco trusted no one, and a few of his friends had been arrested lately for dealing meth. *My bad.* So, he was starting to write down dates, times, and who he sold to as a sort of historical record. If he were to get busted by the police, he could easily go back and see who set him up and deal with them personally. Now, he wanted my first and last name, even asking to photograph my license—which, if I gave it to him, would clearly show Richard Kimble.

He jotted my name down but didn't press me to hand over my ID. He then led me to the kitchen, which was even smaller than the living room. Taco grabbed a small black bag and held it up.

"Check this shit out, man!"

Taco looked in the bag, and a visible panic washed over his face. Then rage. His fist tightened around the bag as he stormed out of the kitchen and into the living room, bellowing at the top of his lungs.

"WHERE THE FUCK IS IT?"

"MOTHERFUCKER!"

"WHERE THE FUCK IS IT, BRO?"

Taco's roommate turned from his seat at the small computer desk while a woman emerged from the back hallway to witness the spectacle.

"Calm down, man!" the roommate shouted, which prompted Taco to lunge forward, grab his roommate's neck, and begin to choke him.

"TELL ME WHERE IT IS!"

The roommate's face turned red until every vein in his neck and forehead was bulging. He then spit and choked out, "I don't know what you're talking about!"

The "it" in question was a giant meth crystal—several ounces in one solid chunk—an over-glorified status symbol in the drug world.

Realizing his meth crystal had been broken up and sold—making it impossible for him to brag about it to me or any of the women he brought into his house—Taco went berserk. He pulled the handgun from his waistband and pushed it into his roommate's chest.

"WELL, IT DIDN'T JUST WALK OFF!" he bellowed.

He flung his body on top of his roommate, toppling him to the ground, punching him with one hand and using his other to beat the guy with the pistol. The woman yelled at the two to stop as two large Dobermans pushed through the crowd and began biting the men's legs. I remained calm as the shitshow unraveled. At one point, I laughed into my listening device to clarify it was just two roommates fighting, aware that an army of officers, already on edge about this deal, was now hearing nothing but screaming and shit breaking. I lied to myself, believing that I had this under control, and I let them know it too.

For fuck's sake, I thought. *Do not ruin this for me by coming in here.*

The roommate finally got a hand free and knocked the pistol from Taco's grasp. As Taco scrambled around the living room, trying to find his gun, his roommate stood up from the mess and grabbed a butcher knife from the computer desktop. Taco didn't notice immediately, but he figured it out when I calmly laughed into my listening device again, mentioning that the roommate now had a knife. Taco found his gun in the mess of couch cushions and pointed it at the roommate, holding as they squared off.

I think it's important to discuss just how bad this situation was beyond these two men trying to kill each other. Again, I was bound by several rules, but I was also living and operating in a world where rules and laws were never followed. Just because I was dressed and presenting as a meth head (truthfully, at this point, I was more of a junkie than a cop) didn't mean I was free from the responsibilities of a police officer. I was sworn to act to save everyone from serious injury or death, even if it meant using deadly force and exposing my undercover identity. There were strict policies in place that were very clear. As a uniformed officer, I would have ended this threat by shooting Taco the instant he put the gun to his roommate's chest. The same went for the roommate as he tried to stab Taco. If either of these men seriously injured or killed the other while I was in the room, I would be held legally responsible. That meant I would be fired, then prosecuted with felony charges and a severe prison sentence.

I barreled toward the two men, who were just a few feet apart and on the verge of killing each other. I jumped between them, risking my own life. I lunged past the roommate, narrowly missing the point of his knife as he swiped wildly back and forth, just inches from my face and chest. I lifted up my knee, ready to kick him in the stomach if he got any closer. As I faced the knife attacks, I backed up to push Taco towards the front door while grabbing his gun with my free hand, pushing it towards the ground so that neither the roommate nor myself would be shot. While marching Taco backward, I felt the wind from the roommate's knife swipes as he screamed wildly and closed in on us. Taco reached over my shoulder, continuing to point his gun at his roommate but unable to shoot as I kept pulling his arm down. Feeling for the door behind me, I managed to unlock the deadbolts and force us safely out onto the porch.

Once outside, Taco caught a second wind of courage and pointed his gun at the roommate again, determined to shoot him for even thinking of trying to stab him. Of course, that meant I was still in a position of potentially getting shot. The fight escalated until my one, perfectly-timed, last move: once the roommate's knife was lowered for just a split second, I shoved him with both hands as hard as I could, knocking him to the living room floor. Before he could get up, I slammed the security door shut and leaned into it with every ounce of energy I could muster. Enraged, the roommate screamed from the other side of the door and kicked it, trying to force it back open.

By this point, I was fully pissed off. Intermittently, the roommate would force the door open only for me to slam it back closed. Frustrations grew, and the roommate began to stab at my palms through the metal grate of the door as I desperately dodged the strikes to keep it closed. The knife would occasionally catch on the diamond pattern of the grate, forcing the roommate to work to free it. Taco pushed my body against the house's entrance in sheer anger as his threats to kill the roommate flew frantically. With one last forceful strike of the knife, the blade got caught in the metal material, permanently entangling it in the door. Both men finally wore out and stopped to catch their breath. Now that I could be heard, they were forced to listen to reason, allowing me to negotiate a truce.

Many people watch the evening news and see the countless murders within our cities and think, maybe the killing was planned. More likely than not, those homicides are actually something closer to what happened with Taco. All too often, they revolve around a dispute over some small dope deal, and rage blocks out consequences for their actions. Taco or his roommate should've died that day, but they're still alive because Ricky was there to stop the impulsive assault and save them from themselves. But also because I was so lost in my environment that I didn't break my cover to shoot either one of them.

I pressed the two to talk it out, leading the conversation so that the fight wouldn't resume. Pieces of my true self always came through in moments like that. After all, the best undercovers just took their best traits and amplified them. Problem-solving, mixed with plenty of humor and talking shit, was in full effect as I talked them down. I knew I could talk this out when I saw Taco tuck his handgun into his waistband (though it was mostly to keep from drawing even more attention from the neighbors). These dudes were violent felons, and there were plenty of guns inside, so it was best to get everyone to calm down. Nobody wanted the cops to come knocking.

I backed away from the door and stood next to Taco, laughing about how I couldn't believe I'd gotten between the two of them. As both men, still panting hard, began laughing, Taco made his way inside the house, and the roommates finally bumped fists.

I could play this day out a dozen times, and the scary part is I know that I would never have broken my cover. My mind's perception of what was actually occurring was broken. I laughed during most of the buy, a clash that very well could have ended in multiple deaths, including my own. My ability to accurately read the danger level had been skewed from years of overriding human instincts. I constantly lived at a heightened sense of danger, so this all seemed very normal to me, which meant that if there were a threat scale of 1–10, I was constantly living at an 8 or 9. And while this situation was definitely a 10, I actually perceived it to be closer to a 4. This also prevented my surveillance team from barging in and halting the entire shitshow. I'd trained them to believe that Ricky could fucking handle anything, which couldn't have been further from the truth.

My phone vibrated like crazy in my front pocket. Frank had been calling repeatedly, trying to understand what in the actual fuck was happening. Understandably, I had been so busy and in the zone that I hadn't even noticed. They'd likely seen Taco pointing a gun at me in the front yard but didn't know I was trying to talk the situation out rather than run. Had I left, one of those dudes—or both—would definitely have ended up dead.

I finally answered my phone. The only thing I heard was Frank barking from the other end, "Hey, dumbass, what the fuck are you doing? Get the fuck out of there—*now*!"

Already gone.

Once I was back in the car, I noticed some kind of intense feeling, but my body didn't react like I'd just been in the middle of a gun and knife fight. I felt great, energized, and fucking excited. It was like I'd just experienced sex for the first time, and I wanted to go at it again. I'd come to learn that this is similar to what drug addicts feel. The problem is that a dopamine rush swings like a pendulum. It doesn't just go back to its usual baseline when the dust settles. The body's dopamine crashes just as hard as it rises, causing a terrible depressive state.

I drove half a block away, then gave approval for the

search warrant on Taco's house. With the house still in sight, I watched a convoy of police cars and tactical vans race down the street past me. I would later learn that Taco kicked out a boarded window in the back of his house to attempt his escape. He'd foolishly made his fortress *too* good and had trapped himself inside his own home. The only thing he could do in the end was throw three guns out of the partially broken window before he was handcuffed. He'd been caught, and our dealings had come to an end.

My day would not end there, though. I would go on to ride the adrenaline spike and complete several buys. While I really needed my supervisor to pull me for the day, I would have fought that decision harder than I fought to keep that door shut while almost being stabbed in the hands. Remember that dopamine pendulum? I couldn't comprehend it, but my body knew what would come if I were to go to the office or sit at home—withdrawal.

In the following weeks, Taco would be in federal court and receive a copy of his discovery, meaning he would have access to all of the evidence we'd built up against him so that his lawyers could form a proper defense. It didn't take long for Taco to forward my reports to his associates to find out who "Ricky" was. My name and excerpts of the reports were flashed all over Facebook where I was labeled "a rat." Even in prison, inmates have social media, and they use it to network with their criminal associates and stoke rumors, sometimes even labeling innocent people "snitches."

Because Taco was associated with almost every meth head on Kansas City's east side, I knew this meant things could potentially get quite tough for me. An army of malicious, hypervigilant tweakers with unlimited time on their hands trying to hunt me down. This thrust me into a state of paranoia, leaving me constantly checking my rearview mirror to make sure I wasn't being followed.

When I was off the clock and driving home, I would circle neighborhoods off the beaten path for miles, acutely aware of surrounding cars, never taking the same route twice. Often, I would park on the interstate and watch every car as it passed me, noting every distinct detail of each vehicle to ensure I wasn't being followed. I never did catch anyone following me, but for the first time, something that resembled fear had been injected into my routine.

My time as an undercover should have been over right there. I was burned out and clearly displaying a serious problem in my ability to read my surroundings. But our division was pressed for doing more with less, and stats were driving our activity. It didn't help that those who should have been saving me from myself were broken as well. We were like a bunch of heroin junkies. It was as if I had just survived fentanyl poisoning, but instead of getting clean and living a normal life, I decided the solution would be to stick to using oxy pills, if you will. So, with this, I changed my car, my undercover name, shaved my dreads off, and I kept out of the east side meth world for a month or so. That was fine until I could no longer fight off my relapse and dove headfirst back into the game.

I'd proven that I could diffuse a deadly situation, which

only poured gasoline on the already raging fire of my overconfidence. Months of vacillating between neuroticism and pride left me with one binary choice: get my head right and go all-in on work again or have a fucking breakdown and lose it all. If there was any sign that my work pace was slowing down, I'd have time to sit in my shit and reflect on what I'd experienced. That's when the ghosts would come back to haunt me.

So, I avoided this by piling on the work. More cases and longer hours meant this day would be buried deep in my psyche and tucked away, never to be heard of again. But what I know now is that trauma is cumulative. This bill would come due at some point, and the longer it was left unaddressed, the higher the interest would be.

CHAPTER 13
MISSING THE BADGE

During my earliest days on the department, I expected surveillance shifts to look like they did in movies: an undercover cop sitting in the car until the subject comes into view, a thrilling moment of instigation after the tension is built, followed by an action-packed high-speed chase or a fight scene until the suspect is caught.

However, in real life, surveillance didn't look like that. The job was more about keeping a low profile and staying in the shadows, which was hard for me, given that I was accustomed to operating with high levels of adrenaline pumping through my body. I mostly hated the mind-numbing hours that would pass while I sat and watched a person's house, waiting to witness any sign of illegal activity so I could determine the most opportune time to send in the SWAT team. And I fucking *despised* the fact that others were off conducting buys—or worse, napping—leaving me with no meal or bathroom breaks, forcing me to get creative by pissing in a bottle.

There was never a time throughout my undercover career that I didn't have a Gatorade bottle in my car, prepped and ready for when I couldn't hold it any longer.

While working surveillance, it was common for people to come and question who I was and why I was parked on their street, especially as a white dude in some of the most Black, gang-infested areas of our city. There was no telling what kinds of characters would knock on my window. Buyers, dealer lookouts, and sometimes just concerned homeowners were the most common types to approach me during these shifts—the latter usually at their wit's end with gang and drug activity in the area.

I got chased off properties several times in my early days of surveillance, but I never took it personally. In the beginning, I had a lot of empathy for these residents. I would apologize and respectfully leave, finding it both amusing and a little sad that they'd never know I was actually working on their behalf—addressing criminal activity in the area and trying to liberate their block from the issues drug dealers created.

In hindsight, I see that Ricky's interactions with others evolved from kind, warm, and funny to abrupt, intense, and explicit. My ability to empathize with the average citizen had waned significantly; I rarely felt guilt when they'd confront the scraggly, dirty shitbag parked outside their house with a look of terror in their eyes. Instead, I caused a scene and berated them if they asked me to move my van. I loved to instigate fights, even knowing the consequences on the streets; by that point, I'd adopted the logic that backing down from a brawl or apologizing made you a weak bitch. The more I grew into Ricky, the more I would live by this code. But these incidents of disrespect caused dozens of homicides in Kansas City each year.

One cold Missouri morning, I parked along a street just one block away from Independence Avenue, watching a meth house to determine the best time for our SWAT team to descend upon it with the warrant we'd procured. Temperatures in the low twenties would make it difficult to be discreet while parked. Normally, I would have shut my engine off to avoid drawing attention to myself and my piping exhaust fumes drifting skyward. But, on this occasion, the joints in my hands were frozen and sore, my cheeks felt raw, and my teeth chattered. I couldn't handle the bone-chilling temperature any longer, so I revved my engine and turned up the heat.

Meanwhile, I watched the home through my rearview mirror, leading any potential lookouts to believe I was not there to bust them. In time, the door to the house I was watching swung open, and I saw three unsightly characters amble down the front steps before migrating in the direction of my car. I observed them intently, straining to see if any of the three matched the suspect I was looking for. But as they came into view, I realized they were just random losers aimlessly walking around.

The group slowly walked up behind my car, seemingly oblivious to their surroundings, while I tried to remain as inconspicuous as possible. I knew I'd accomplished this once the group had pressed past my vehicle without any obvious care that I was there at all. Then, suddenly, I was caught off guard by someone else.

Bang!

I jumped, blood rushing to my head, pulse throbbing in my ears, as the man who'd slammed his palm up against my driver's side window had my full attention. The blast had startled me so much that I thought it was a gunshot. He proceeded to slam his palms into the driver's side window until the three walkers up the street turned to watch the situation unfold.

Believing I could drive away from the angry guy who was now sneering at me through the window, I turned away as if I couldn't hear him. This behavior only incited a more grandiose outburst from the man. I picked up my phone and called another detective, thinking the guy might be deterred by seeing me make a phone call. Instead, the man's eyes widened with fury as the veins in his neck bulged.

"Why the FUCK are you outside my house?!" the guy bellowed, pounding his fist on the top of my car. I could only stare straight ahead as he proceeded to pace the length of my vehicle, intermittently jamming his booted heels into my door.

"YOU STUPID FUCK! GET THE FUCK OUT OF HERE!" he continued.

This went on for several minutes as my adrenaline surged; then, suddenly, I felt myself physiologically shift into Ricky. Fury spread through my veins, my surroundings momentarily blurred, and my fists clenched.

"Get your fucking hands off my van, you stupid fuck! Don't touch my shit again!" I yelled while manually cranking down the window. The man launched back with the same ferocity.

"YOU'RE NOT GONNA FUCKING YELL AT ME IN FRONT OF MY HOUSE!" he barked.

As the man and I continued to exchange insults, I reached for the small radio I kept tucked between my legs to attempt to notify our SWAT team, hoping they would hear the issue and come to my aid. My actions were immediately halted when the man reached one hand behind his back, then pulled out a piece-of-shit black handgun held together by duct tape. He stepped back from the window, lifted the gun, pointed it at my face through my cracked driver's side window, and began taunting me to threaten him again.

"Come on, motherfucker!" he howled. "You won't leave? I'LL FUCKING KILL YOU!"

I'd been in countless life-threatening situations up to that point, but staring down the barrel of a gun still did shit to me.

I paused and took a breath, contemplating how to un-fuck the situation, reaching again for my police radio to alert the squad of my emergency. With my pointer finger digging into the transmission button, I began speaking as loudly and concisely as possible.

"PUT THE GUN DOWN, DUDE. I'll leave, man. Put the gun down. I'm already gone," I urged.

Though this was more for the purpose of the call, my clear directives unexpectedly defused the man. He backed away slowly, proceeding to hurl expletives at me. Once I was clear to drive away, I rolled forward and noticed that we'd attracted quite a bit of attention from onlookers who'd streamed out of the nearby houses, their cell phones out, recording the incident. I made it past the stop sign at the end of the block, then turned up my radio volume and gave a briefing to the squad.

"All right, guys. Dude was unhappy that I was parked near his house and put a gun in my face. You'll need two teams when you hit this house: one to go after the guy who almost blew my head off and the other for the warrant," I informed them.

"We're on it; two minutes away," a voice affirmed through the radio.

I would later learn that the SWAT team who knocked on his door was immediately met with the same aggression I'd just witnessed. Apparently, the man was pissed about having his door nearly beaten down, only to open it and be greeted by several guns (go figure).

The officers proceeded to de-escalate the situation and, upon questioning the man, learned he was especially irritated that meth users were always leaving needles in his yard or parking out front of his house. I could glean from his sentiment that he thought I'd been another user, drawing attention to his property, and that our argument had been the guy's breaking point.

In a way, I felt responsible. To a degree, Ricky had perpetuated the situation, providing yet another example of how Brent's relationship with reality was dissolving inside my work identity. Things I would have never said or done as Brent, I was more than willing to do or say as Ricky. This wasn't limited to my on-the-job risky buys or operations; it also extended to my actions outside of work. Ricky regularly made an appearance in my tone and body language—he was rough, pushy, and swore a lot.

I made life pretty unbearable for my family during this time. Wesley often said it wasn't what I said but how I said it—simple things, such as giving her directions to somewhere she wasn't familiar with or answering her questions about what the orthodontist had said about our daughter's braces. My responses would be short and clipped, as if she should know these things without me having to tell her. We'd get horrified glances from educators and PTA members at school functions as I unknowingly dropped "fuck" in almost every sentence. I could sense how much these parents wanted their kids to stay away from mine. *And who could blame them?* I sure as hell wouldn't want my child being corrupted by some slimeball who was always skulking around at daddy-daughter dances looking like a haggard mess.

I would also catch negative responses while shopping or going out to eat. While shopping at Target, I was followed by a security guard who tried to hide at the end of the aisle. I wouldn't ignore this blatant action and confronted him with, "What in the fuck do you want, motherfucker?"

I then began to notice Wesley and I only being seated at tables near the bathroom or kitchen when we went out together. Ricky would come roaring out as I yelled at one hostess for the slight, demanding a different seat. Had I more control, I would have used some charm and manners and definitely been accommodated. But the way I went off embarrassed Wesley so much that she immediately left for the car, abandoning our night out. My loss of impulse control is easy to see now, but it wasn't in the moment. Back then, I was a violent tornado tearing through the very fabric of our lives.

Being fucking filthy, in every way imaginable and at all times, often caused me to miss the proud feeling of wearing a polished police uniform. Not necessarily because I was appreciative to be a part of the blue family, but because that crisp uniform and clean crew cut showed the world that I was a "good guy" who chased and locked up criminals versus filthy, lawless Ricky who was only out for a high. Though what I was doing was far more impactful for the citizens of Kansas City, I never felt that way because I only saw Ricky in the mirror.

This would begin to negatively impact my self-esteem and make me panic that I could never reclaim my identity as a "good guy." In turn, I began looking for creative ways to interject myself into scenarios as "the police." The problem was that Ricky had two-foot-long dreadlocks at this point—no law-abiding citizen would have believed that I was part of the force, nor would they have trusted me to be a safe person.

On one day in particular, I was sitting in my undercover car, bored, watching a house that was about to be hit by SWAT, when I noticed a police helicopter circling over my vehicle. After several minutes, I realized they were looking for something bad, given their flight patterns. Upon switching my radio to the chopper's frequency, I asked the group if they were looking for a suspect, when suddenly, a man's head poked out from a nearby row of messy shrubs. The man peered up in the sky, then waited for the helicopter to pass before migrating down the block to the next nearest set of scraggly bushes.

I kept my eyes on him while in communication with the helicopter and learned that the man had been in a high-speed chase in a stolen car, wrecked the vehicle with a baby inside, then escaped on foot. I helped to direct the helicopter and the patrol cars to the place where he was hiding.

Within minutes, sirens blared from every direction. Officers swarmed the neighborhood, setting up several blocks of barricades. The moment the man heard the sirens, he shot off, running through front yards and slithering down alleyways between houses to throw off the squad. I proceeded to follow the man in my car as strategically as possible. I watched as police tried to follow him on foot, noticing two heftier, gray-haired officers struggling to keep up with their suspect.

There's nothing I love more than a good foot chase, I reminisced. During my days in blue, I was a sub-five-minute miler and would fuck with a running suspect by waiting until they got tired, ensuring they were out of fight by the time I pushed them to the ground. In this instance, I aimed to do something similar. I rolled over to the next block, where the subject was headed via a back alley. My plan was to drive up beside the guy, then coast for several feet until my driver's door was parallel with the man, at which time I'd knock him to the ground by opening my car door real hard. My goal was to then park the car and hold him until the portly uniformed officers could catch up.

In no time, the suspect rounded the corner of the nearby alleyway; neither pudgy officer was in sight by that point. I proceeded to speed up my car toward the subject, prompting him to fall on the ground, arms spread forward in a position of full surrender. He appeared to be giving up.

Though I'd initially envisioned getting out of the car and tackling the guy, something in my gut told me it was a bad idea. Instead, I sat there, frozen in my car, staring down a suspect through my driver's window as he kept making eye contact with me, his face twisting with obvious confusion as to why I wasn't jumping out after him. This strange, wordless, adrenaline-packed exchange delayed him just enough to be spotted by one of the officers who was now breathlessly tearing down the block in our direction.

When it occurred to the subject that I wasn't trying to arrest him, he stood up and proceeded to make his escape. It was then that I had a radical epiphany: I wasn't wearing a uniform. I *looked like* the suspect. Ricky *looked like* the streets. In this dynamic, we had something in common I could use as leverage.

I then rolled down the windows of my car, made direct eye contact with the guy, and yelled, "HURRY! GET IN, MAN! LET'S GO."

He ran over to my front passenger door, and I began locking my driver's side door, pretending I was trying to unlock the passenger door. The man yanked on the handle, desperately trying to unlock it, bellowing, "LET ME IN! C'MON, MAN! LET ME IN!"

"Pull the handle!" I commanded through the closed car door. "Hurry the fuck up, the cops are close! Get the fuck in!"

I watched him struggle, smirking internally, brainstorming other ways I could keep him occupied.

"Try the back door!" I yelled and pointed.

The man scrambled to the back door as I began pushing

the lock button over and over. He then escalated to panic and tore over to my side of the vehicle. Though I expected him to try to open the driver's side door, I watched him stall, gazing toward the sidewalk, his eyes widening with fear. I then glanced in the direction he was facing and realized the officer was now standing near my headlights, pointing his gun at me.

It was weird—that officer had no way of knowing we were on the same team. But I looked at him all pissed off as if to say, *What the fuck, man? Don't point that shit at me*! I lifted my hands over my head, making sure to comply so I would not get shot by friendly fire. The suspect, on the other hand, attempted to flee like a fucking idiot and was caught a few feet past my taillights.

A struggle ensued between them as the suspect tried to escape the officer's grip on his arm. I watched as the tired officers started to struggle in an all-out street brawl with the suspect. Running on sheer adrenaline, and without a second thought, I jumped out of my vehicle and charged at the two as they fought. As I did, the suspect looked in my direction, an expression of relief on his face; I could only assume he thought I was about to help him fight off the cop and escape, but he was mistaken.

"Ten-eighty-one! Ten-eighty-one!" I yelled to indicate to the cop that I was a fellow officer. At this, he pulled back, allowing me to tackle the suspect to the ground, lock him in a figure-four leg lock, and apply plenty of pain compliance. The officer gave me a grateful wave, sidled up to me as I held the suspect down, reached for his handcuffs, and then locked them around the suspect's wrists. Meanwhile, the suspect glanced at me with contempt in his eyes, hating me for tricking him.

Enter Ricky, who just couldn't fucking help but be snide.

"Gotcha, bitch," I said, the sides of my mouth curling into a satisfied smile as I patted the suspect on the shoulder. "Better luck next time, fuckwad."

I then looked over at the cop.

"You good, bro?" I asked.

"Yeah, thanks for your help, man," he said.

"You got it, and—just for the record, dude—I was never here." He gave an affirmative nod as I darted away, trying to avoid drawing too much attention from onlookers who might later recognize me.

That evening, I drove away, warmed by nostalgia about how good it felt to—momentarily—be "back in action" as the "real police." I was also affirmed that my skills were actually put to better use as an undercover than a uniformed officer in this scenario. The experience helped to ease the mental confusion brought on by years of living two different lives.

Ricky was here to stay. But on that day, I didn't feel like such a piece of shit for being him. I was reminded that the work I was doing was valuable and for the greater good—even if it mostly didn't feel like it.

CHAPTER 14
SEARCHING FOR SOMETHING MORE

Even with a strong addiction to the adrenaline and work, it is possible to become burned out and feel the need for a change. I found myself in this situation after several years of being an undercover. I decided to take on a new assignment. By this time, I had worked the second-longest undercover tenure ever in the history of our department. My time as an undercover was more than twice the usual length of the job. The extraordinary amount of time I spent as Ricky would make my transition back to normalcy and "real" police work—patrols and anything in uniform—very difficult.

Thankfully, my next assignment was an administrative one in our Drug Enforcement Unit. I was still able to dress down in civilian clothes and continue to work around the narcotics world that strangely felt like home. I can't imagine how difficult it would have been had I been asked to go back into a uniform and work in patrol and interact with the general public. My temper was short, my patience was nonexistent, and I didn't trust anything or anyone. All I could do was imagine someone calling 911 over some bogus dispute, which happened more than you would ever guess, and me losing my shit. Many callers complained about civil, rather than criminal, matters that had nothing to do with the law, just because they wanted a referee of some sort. If that had been my career path, I'm almost sure I would have been fired or quit.

There were challenges with my transition seemingly every day. These problems were mine to carry, but my coworkers and supervisors were placed into just as new of a world having to manage me. Their inability to relate and fully understand the world I had walked in for so many years made working with me a strained task at best.

I would find myself searching for something more in this new work. It was so confusing that I was relieved to be in a place that wasn't nasty and full of danger, but also pissed off that I wasn't able to find any excitement in my work. This would cause me to constantly try to make my cases something they were not. I needed to find anything possible to bring me back to what was normal to me.

I had a sense of being trapped in some sort of dull cubicle hell compared to the freewheeling days of constant go, go, go. I was like someone who had been thrown into a room by themselves to go through withdrawals. Anger and agitation were the easiest things for people to see. But my internal experiences were the ones I would fight even more than my outwardly visible ones.

I had absolutely no insight or awareness that my less-than-pleasant interactions with the world were actually core changes in who I had become as a person. Those changes made it nearly impossible to navigate normal life without looking like an irritable asshole. I was constantly feeling a need to move—staying still for even a few moments would drive me to be simultaneously vigilant about and agitated by my surroundings. This happened even in safe places. I had an ever-growing frustration with people, which was especially volatile when I had to explain something to them.

My attitude towards my coworkers and my supervisor was no exception. They could not understand my thinking and processes and I could not understand how they could be so content in doing such seemingly unimportant and insignificant work. This would cause bigger issues as I continued to struggle. I was depressed, but it was because I needed the action I was so used to. I was angry, because we all worked in the drug world, yet these team members barely knew that world—not like I did. In my mind, they were idiots, and I would talk to them as such, leading to many reprimands and a few write-ups.

I also believed that I had total control over anyone at any time I wanted. I was used to talking my supervisors into letting me do whatever crazy buy or operation I wanted. My sense of control over bad guys, meth heads, heroin addicts, and crack heads was engrained in me, whereas everyone else knew we had no control over these people, only the drugs did. I believed that I had some innate ability to gain control over any situation. This misguided thought was somehow solidified further through my traumas and incidents. Since I never got burned, so to speak, I never had that eye-opening experience to bring the reality of my situations to my active mind. I always seemed to win, so my delusion that I was in control grew. This need to not only have control but curate my own high intensity experiences stayed. Those experiences were now at odds with my new boss and my new environment.

The problem was that I was still living as Ricky, but stashed in an office culture. It reminded me of the feeling I'd been told first responders got when they had to leave their work due to retirement or injury—it felt like a loss of self. It hit hard. I was totally unaware that Ricky wasn't just the clothes, the hair, the slang, and how I walked. The crazy part was that I never picked up on the fact that I had actually *become* Ricky, and this crude, selfish, and impatient addict was not meant to be in an office. I was now built to be in a motel somewhere or in a smoke house getting my fix. Now, I was in a cubicle prison, and Ricky was having none of it.

As I had put on an act to initially become Ricky as a new undercover, I did the same in reverse now. I would put on my best Brent disguise to avoid finding myself in constant trouble. It was such a mindfuck to have to put on a different hat to be the person I once was. And just like when I was a new UC, it felt strange and so foreign to be Brent again. This struggle of flipping back and forth put so much strain on my mind I could barely stand it. I was allegedly in the most stress-free unit in our division, one of the more coveted positions, and I was the most stressed I had ever been. I experienced so much stress that I developed alopecia and my beard hair began falling out along with several spots on my head.

Talk about some shit, right? I wasn't even risking my life anymore, and now I was feeling more stress than when I had a gun to my head? But that was just how it went with undercover work. The stress was no longer in the actual UC work. That was where I had become comfortable. The dangers in that world were invisible to me. I was used to living at a constant eight out of ten on a threat scale. Now, I had been thrust, cold turkey, into a constant two. Feeling nothing was agonizing and the boredom that was my every day hit me with the same effects as withdrawals.

I stayed the course in my new assignment, always trying to make something of nothing. There would always be another case that could get me out of the office and into some real action. But this was not the mode that anyone in my office wanted to perform in. I was all alone and stuck in a world with zero action.

There is something so drastic in moving away from the undercover or covert work life and joining the world of normalcy. By being Ricky, I changed myself to an entirely new person. One that went against all morals I had lived by for more than thirty years. The transition into the undercover world was by far easier than trying to leave it. This difficulty would have me starting to drink more frequently to cope. I also began looking for any chance I could to get back into my life as Ricky. I thought that it must be similar to what prisoners go through when they're released back into society. Most of them have been institutionalized for so long that they think being in prison is better than trying to life a free life. The undercover world, which was full of the worst in society, who Brent would never associate with, was where I wanted to be. I no longer wanted to be Brent. When I should have been trying to rid myself of Ricky, getting rid of Brent and bringing Ricky back was all I could think of. The anticipation of getting my adrenaline fix again and getting back to my people seemed to be my cure. Shockingly, that's exactly how addicts describe what it feels like just thinking about getting high.

CHAPTER 15
JULY 15TH

In early 2018, I'd found just the cure for my struggles, and I took a transfer as an undercover to one of the most elite units in all of Kansas City. They were known as the Gun Squad. Formed in 2009, the unit consisted of only the best detectives and an elite squad of ATF agents. The Gun Squad's mission was to investigate the worst criminals in the Kansas City area and use covert and undercover operations to dismantle the criminal enterprises known for trafficking dope and guns. As the years of successes grew, so did the duties and tasks of these detectives.

The Gun Squad's mission creep led to us being assigned to work with the Homicide Unit, conducting an immediate follow-up whenever a murder occurred. We would pursue the suspect immediately after each killing, using a variety of methods. This squad was originally founded to focus on long-term, large-scale drug and gun undercover buys. However, we were now also tasked with tracking down nearly every murder suspect in the city. For a city that consistently experiences more than 150 murders per year, this placed a heavy workload on our small team.

Working more than eighty hours a week was common during my time with the Gun Squad. Each member was committed to ensuring a safe community by holding criminals accountable. This meant that I was on call around the clock and guaranteed to miss holidays, kids' birthdays, and special family events. I accepted this as part of the price to ensure the worst offenders didn't continue their reign on the streets.

I was handpicked to join the Gun Squad for my dedicated work ethic, my creative thinking during investigations, and my willingness to do anything to win. I also had more undercover experience than anyone in our division. I knew most of the detectives from the few times I'd ventured down the long hall toward their secret offices, where they always hid behind closed doors. This gave me confidence that I could make a great contribution to the team.

By July 2018, a criminal known as Oklahoma's Most Violent Robber had moved to Kansas City and quickly proved that he was worthy of his title. Marlon Mack, sticking to the life he knew, committed armed robberies across the city. In early July, he killed a man in cold blood during a robbery at a fried fish restaurant, and Mack's face was all over the television. Given that he was known by at least half the city, we were confident that we could find Mack and bring him to justice. Little did my squad know that this case would change us all and serve as the *end* of Ricky.

We set out one Monday in rabid search of Mack—first by

looking for his car, a blue Acura, that hadn't been seen all week, then by locating his friends' and girlfriend's houses to determine where he was hiding out.

What many citizens don't realize is that there are times when our homicide unit knows exactly who committed a murder, but they need additional time before an arrest can be made. The necessary processing of witness statements and evidence can't happen overnight. When a case isn't at the point where charges can be filed, arresting the suspect usually results in them being released quickly from custody; then, finding him or her after can be twice as hard.

Another factor is arrest teams and their availability. Our arrest team was the elite tactical unit within the Kansas City Police Department. In plain terms, they were the Navy SEALs of SWAT teams. For as many directions as the Gun Squad was pulled, these guys were twice as busy.

Summers in Kansas City brought murders almost every night. So, the Gun Squad and our SWAT teams were exhausted from chasing down each suspect on top of our usual dope work. Most of us had not had a single day off for a month straight. It often felt like our days never really started, nor did they ever really end—work was just life, and life was just work. So, when the first chance to have a day off came, many took this time to show their families they still existed. A small portion of us decided to continue tracking Mack, but we had to supplement our surveillance numbers with detectives from our Gun Squad.

With a limited number of detectives and only a two-man crew from our tactical unit, it was determined that the weekend we went looking for Mack would be surveillance-only. The usual tactical crew for a suspect like Mack would be a minimum of six team members in three cars to overwhelm him and mitigate a violent encounter. An offender like Mack brought much higher risks of pursuits, fights, and officer-involved shootings. Bringing such a force to the scene dramatically reduced these possibilities while also giving officers the upper hand should the worst-case scenario play out. With our staffing low, the goal was to locate Mack and specifically *not* engage him. By searching for him in a covert manner, we would be able to locate where he was hiding and put the full squad and tactical unit together on Monday morning to arrest him.

On Sunday, July 15, 2018, I prepared to endure a scorching Midwestern summer day while working surveillance. After rifling through the kitchen for a quick snack that I could eat on the road, I approached Wesley, who was sitting on the couch, reading a book, and leaned in to kiss her cheek. I went outside, climbed into the driver's seat of my undercover minivan, then headed to take my spot at Mack's girlfriend Sarah's house. Our hope was that if Mack didn't show up at Sarah's, she could at least lead us to him.

Within thirty minutes, I was parked on Sarah's block, several houses away, with just enough of a view of the property that I could see her front door. Sarah's house sat atop a hill, which made it difficult to park discreetly. Normally, I would have chosen to sit in my car with the sun to my back; that way, anyone looking in my direction would have to fight the glare to see inside my vehicle. That was not the case today, as I had to face east toward the rising sun, so I planned to accommodate for this, too. I shut off my minivan and then crawled over the middle console to get to the furthest row of seats. Then, I crouched down, so anyone peering into my car would think the vehicle was empty. I stayed there for an hour, watching the house. There was no movement—until, finally, a detective's voice broke over the radio: "Hey, guys, there's a blue Acura circling the block over here."

We knew Mack had a blue Acura, which was very rare and especially noticeable in this area, which consisted of beat-to-shit trucks and minivans that made mine look like a showroom model. Though the detective could not get the license plate to confirm that it was Mack, it was suspicious enough that we were convinced it was him.

My radio crackled with constant updates. Two detectives attempted to follow the Acura as it snaked through the narrow, car-lined blocks in the area near Sarah's house. The decision was made to stop following the car, as it would have been obvious that we were doing counter-surveillance. The detectives allowed the Acura to drive away, assuming he might come back. They assumed right.

After about ten minutes of driving with no one following, the blue Acura drove over to Sarah's house. I called out every movement of the car on my radio as I lay low in the back of my minivan.

"The Acura is parked. It's facing west so that he can see me, but I can't see him well as I'm looking straight into the sun," I stated.

The Acura idled for what felt like forever. I squinted and

craned my neck in a way I hoped didn't draw suspicion, but the tint on the windows made it impossible to get a view of the driver.

Damn it.

"Is it Mack? Can you confirm it's him?" a detective asked over the radio.

"Fuck, man, I can't," I answered. I knew whoever it was wasn't looking at me, but that still didn't mean they weren't being rightfully cautious about a van they'd never noticed on their street.

Every surveillance car converged into the area as the squad anticipated the Acura's departure. My role was to watch for anyone getting in or out of the car and to try to identify Mack if I saw him. My eyes strained as I focused intently on the Acura through the binoculars hanging around my neck. In time, the vehicle stopped idling, pulled away from the curb, and drove right past me. I peered into the driver's window less than a foot away, which, again, proved to be impossible to see through as the tint was too dark.

The Acura cut through the neighborhood slowly, making several deliberate turns. This confirmed among the squad that the suspect *had* to be Mack—his driving was indicative of someone checking for surveillance. Trying to remain as covert as possible, our team proceeded to trail him, lose him, then pick his car up again. The Acura finally turned into a small parking lot outside a shithole on the east side called the Sky-Vu motel, which was flanked by a tall privacy fence. The spot was known as a hiding place for criminals, as its management had a history of being unwilling to cooperate with the police.

When a detective called out over the radio that the Acura

was pulling into the Sky-Vu parking lot, I knew we were about to be done for the day. This would be where he would hole up for the night and we'd catch him on Monday, bright and early. The radio buzzed with ideas and suggestions on how to determine which room he was in. Some of the squad even petitioned for us to call off surveillance for the day.

I always needed the heavy lifting to be on my shoulders, and I always needed a victory over the bad guy. There would be no leaving until we knew exactly what room Mack would be in. I got on the radio and immediately formulated a plan, on the fly, per usual.

My idea was to have another detective pick me up and drop me off out of sight near the Sky-Vu parking lot. This would ensure I could walk up to the motel without raising any red flags. Once I was inside Sky-Vu's office, I planned to haggle the manager into giving me a room for the night so I could keep watch over Mack's motel room and Acura. There seemed to be no pushback from the group on my intentions. They knew this was Ricky's sweet spot, and frankly, I think they were grateful they weren't the ones that had to go in on foot. Like I'd ever give them the chance to get a fix.

Around five minutes later, I parked my van about a half-mile from the motel to wait for my colleague, Brian, who would be giving me a ride to my drop-off point. While I waited for him, I worked on looking the part: pulling on my most meth-looking outfit, with sparkling skulls and oversized shorts. I hot-boxed a few cigarettes for a tobacco-infused smell and started doing pushups to bring a hard sweat on. Simultaneously, arrangements were made by the squad to keep another colleague, Detective Riley, on a running call via my cell phone that would be muted on his end so that he could relay what was happening to the group without the threat of blowing my cover. Then, I looked down at my Glock. *I should probably take this thing,* I thought. *But where on my body would I hide it?*

This was a weird thing to consider because I had exclusively been without my gun on all undercover operations for more than three years. Ricky just didn't carry a gun. On this day, however, for a split second I contemplated bringing it. I took the Glock from my dashboard, looked it over, and considered how I could hide it beneath my undercover gear. My mind was then flooded with scenarios of what would happen if I had an altercation with Mack and my gun was exposed too soon; so, I determined it was best to leave it behind.

While en route to the motel with Brian, I called Riley, ensured he could hear me, and had him mute his end. Within minutes, Brian rolled up to our drop-off spot and parked near the shoulder of the highway. My parting words were asking him where he was parking so that I knew where to go upon leaving. Brian promised to wait for me well out of sight in the neighborhood behind the motel.

I got out of the car and began walking toward Sky-Vu, intermittently picking up dust with my hands to rub all over my shirt and shorts. I'd seen this parking lot hundreds of times, but now that I was on foot in it, I could see how small it really was. The shallow lot was so cramped that most cars chose to back onto the highway instead of doing the three-point turn it took to turn around to leave.

I immediately caught sight of the blue Acura parked

alongside the north building. As I made my way over to the manager's office, I knew my biggest challenge would be haggling with him. I paced to the front steps of the motel and pushed open the glass door to step inside.

I didn't even have the chance to wince at the half-dozen plug-in air fresheners in this tiny space when I was hammered with an unexpected adrenaline dump. The door jammed on the uneven floor and only opened halfway, forcing me to squeeze through the tiny opening to the right, where Mack was seated. His feet blocked my path, causing me to step over them as I noticed he was neurotically texting on two cell phones. Suddenly, the eight-by-ten-foot room seemed even smaller. Without missing a beat, I stepped right into my role.

"Sup." I nodded at Mack, walking up to the manager's desk, which was encased by bulletproof glass. The desk behind the glass was empty, so I rang the service bell over and over, then shoved my hands into my pockets while letting out an irritated huff. I wanted to sell Mack on the fact that I was just a random meth head looking for a place to stay. So, I paced the room, then, when no one appeared at the desk after a full minute, I returned to the bell and, as annoyingly as possible, continued ringing it.

Ding-ding-ding!

I nonchalantly pulled out my phone and held it in my palm so Riley could hear my exchanges with Mack.

I observed Mack's movements in the reflection of the glass, keeping a vigilant watch over him so he wouldn't come up and execute me as he had his last victim. I turned to him with an annoyed tone and canted my head at the desk.

"You seen this dude?"

Mack only glared at me—not even acknowledging my question—and the glare felt like a punch. I could tell something was off with him. I know my brain picked up on these sinister nonverbal cues, but I pushed those aside as I always did. My hypervigilance and need to win sent me into overdrive. I saw a window that seemed almost too easy. This was a more-than-perfect opportunity to arrest Mack.

He's away from his car, inside a bulletproof box with only one way out, I estimated. *He's trapped*. That was all the thinking I did, and I called an audible, deciding this was the best place to end his run on the streets. I acted pissed off about the absent manager, then stormed past Mack. He purposefully left his outstretched legs where they were in the way.

The only thing left to do was to call the small arrest team and tell them to wait Mack out at the door. I figured we could capture Mack before he made it to his car. I grabbed my cell phone to tell Riley the new plan, but my phone only showed a blank screen.

Goddammit, I thought to myself. My phone had lost signal, and the call had been dropped.

The department had just switched my undercover phone over to a shitty carrier, which was known for having huge blocks of straight-up dead zones and zero coverage, which left me all alone more often than not. I had no idea how long the line had been dead. I aimed to get to a place outside where I could detail my new plan. I shuffled down the stairs, then out into the parking lot where I, as discreetly as possible, made a call to Riley to discuss the arrest plan. I dialed the number, only to be met with a *beep, beep, beep*: the call wouldn't go through. Now pissed off, I tried again, only to be met with the same irritating sound. Suddenly, I heard the manager shouting at me from the step, asking if I was the guy who'd been ringing the desk bell.

I shoved my phone back into my pocket, then approached him. Through the front glass door, I could see Mack intently watching our interaction. There, just off the front steps of the hotel, I carried out my plan of haggling with the manager to get a cheap room for the night. While speaking with the man, Riley and I texted about sending in our arrest team immediately. I held my pointer finger up in the manager's bulbous face, mouthing, *one minute*, then stepped away from our conversation. Once out of earshot, I murmured the arrest plan to Riley and told him to hurry them the fuck up. I then returned to bargaining with the manager.

I would find out later that the two homicide detectives assigned to this case neglected to tell our squad that on Friday they'd gone to Sarah's house and asked her questions about Mack and his whereabouts. That would have been good to know and may have changed how I'd proceeded. Sarah also had a high-quality surveillance camera system, which she used to take photos of the detectives, and she had sent them to Mack via text message. What I found out later was that all the attention Mack gave to his phone, while I was a few feet away from him, was his paranoia. He was sitting there trying to compare the homicide detective's photo with me. As I was stalking him, I didn't realize he was stalking me, too.

"No, bro," I argued. "There's no way in hell you're selling me a room in this shithole for sixty." I acted flustered to play the part, then stormed away, keeping an eye on the Acura the entire time as I jaunted across the asphalt. I kept Riley on the open line, pleading with him to send the arrest team faster.

It only took a minute for the SWAT car to come into view on the horizon. I felt relieved as I'd been anxiously asking Riley every five seconds where the hell they were. I now saw the arrest team's car screaming down the highway toward Sky-Vu. I took my eyes off the road only for a second to see Mack walking out of the office to his vehicle, which caused my stomach to drop.

"I need the guys to hurry. Mack's leaving the office. Give the team a heads-up. They need to catch him before he gets to his car," I urged Riley via text.

"They're coming, man!" Riley responded.

My heart rate quickened. The plan was in full motion; there would be no calling it off. The odds of this bet had suddenly shifted out of our favor.

The blue Acura was parked with its bumper facing the building—positioned perfectly for trapping and coaxing out a target.

Mack slowly paced through the parking lot, focusing on his two cell phones, never looking up or showing any indication of nervousness. The unmarked, navy-blue Ford Explorer carrying two tactical officers zipped into the parking lot just as Mack made it back to his vehicle. He stood beside the driver's side door, eyeing the police car as it sped towards him and screeched to a halt just feet from his rear bumper. He remained eerily calm, as it was clear the police car was there to arrest him. Mack opened his car door, slid into the driver's seat, and he slowly pulled the door closed.

Still standing near the side of the road, I watched the two extremely skilled and well-respected tactical officers, whom I had worked alongside every day for years, exit their police SUV, guns drawn, demanding that Mack exit the car. The way the situation played out made no sense to me.

Mack's wanted for murder—he knows the police are here for him, yet he's showing no panic and not trying to flee the scene?

In a matter of seconds, the passenger door of Mack's car flung open, and out stepped a man whom none of us had noticed was sitting inside Mack's vehicle. The passenger raised his hands over his head as he slowly sidestepped away from the Acura.

"STEP BACK TOWARDS THE SOUND OF MY VOICE!" one of the officers called out.

The passenger ignored this command, which signaled to me that we were going to have a problem. Never once in my time as an undercover had I inserted myself into a takedown. This day would be the first time I felt compelled to assist the two tactical officers on the scene, and it would prove to be the greatest mistake of my career.

Almost involuntarily, I hurried across the tiny parking lot and approached Mike, the SWAT officer at the driver's door of the police car. He was positioned behind his open door, pointing a gun at the Acura. Mike had been a member of one of my original cover crews, having been in his elite unit around the same time that I was first assigned as an undercover.

"Dude, it's Ricky. I need a gun," I told him. "I don't have one."

Mike glanced at me, responding simply, "No." He was

obviously focused on Mack, and he sure as hell was not expecting Ricky to walk up to his back during the takedown of such a violent suspect. His initial thought had to be, *What the hell is this random tweaker doing?* It wasn't uncommon to have some mentally ill or high passerby approach the police during a takedown. But to realize that Ricky was on his ass, diverting his attention while he was completing the task I'd asked for was just not normal.

I scanned Mike's open car, astonished that the seats weren't loaded with all kinds of weapons. The only additional gun Mike had on him was an AR that was locked into a rifle holder. It'd been so long since I'd been near a police car that I would've never been able to unlock and retrieve that rifle on my own.

My attention shifted. Through Mike's windshield, I could see the passenger from the Acura still slowly side-stepping away from the car, not following the commands of Mike's partner, Patrick. Determined to help the pair, I decided I would take control of the passenger and detain him so that Patrick and Mike could focus all of their attention on Mack, ultimately giving them a two-on-one advantage. However, I was dressed as Ricky, meaning I had no cuffs, vest, or badge, making this a bit more difficult.

I eyed the handcuffs on Mike's belt and decided to swipe them when suddenly, a large *BOOM!* forced my instincts to kick in and throw me into a crouching stance as gravel from the parking lot and metal from the car door exploded around me. I immediately knew it was gunfire, and we were under attack.

This was only the beginning of what Mack had in store for us.

Mack exited the Acura, his AK-47 roaring—rounds screamed from the barrel as he targeted Mike, Patrick, and me. Suddenly, my surroundings began to melt together as though I was in some kind of fever dream. My perception of reality was completely fragmented by shock. The bullet barrage continued to pin me down and I couldn't tell where Mack was. I stayed low to the ground and noticed the taste of gunpowder on my tongue as my instincts took over. Now, this is the crazy part. I clearly remember coming up with no less than a dozen moves. Time was standing still, so it should have been impossible for me to formulate so many plans in the second it took.

I stood up to move to cover behind Mike's car when I looked over and observed him lying belly down on the ground. I thought he was dead. All I knew was that he had a gun, and if I didn't get to him, Mack would likely run up and put several more rounds in him, execution style. I started to make a move for Mike's gun. The bullets continued zipping through the air, causing pavement and metal from the open driver's door to fly in my face. I was then shocked when Mike jumped up from the ground and, in an instant, we both moved to the back of the police SUV for cover.

Just as I was about to round the corner of the bumper, I tripped—my left leg buckled, sending me rolling to the ground. I did a somersault and landed in a crouched position facing Mack, who was now running full steam towards Mike and me, hammering the trigger of his gun. I stayed in a bear crawl position, facing the direction of the bullets with no cover and no gun to protect myself.

Again, I pictured ways to escape from this situation without being shot. The echoes of gunshots ricocheted off of every surface, making it difficult to determine where Mack was. At this point, everything became really quiet, like someone had hit the mute button. I lowered my body and peeked beneath the SUV, seeing if I could spot Mack's feet beneath the police car. Plumes of smoke and dust billowed from every part of the parking lot as I searched for our target. Suddenly, an object clipped my right calf; when I looked down, my leg wasn't gushing blood, so I assumed it must have been a rock or shrapnel. This sudden shock sped everything up and brought the full volume back to my senses. I surmised that Mack had a pretty good view of me, given how hard I'd been struck by the object. I knew I had to move, but all that would do was make me a vulnerable target.

Eyeing the parameters of the Sky-Vu lot, I noticed Mike and Patrick high-tailing it east. I would come to find out they were redirecting and attempting to flank Mack to attack him from a different angle. I knew I had to move. I was in a terrible position and was more exposed than not.

I scanned the parking lot one last time to ensure my safety, but I was horrified to see that Mack had me in his sights. Large flames were now spitting out the end of his rifle, which he was now aiming directly at me. My primal instinct to flee took over, and I stood up, turned, and began running through the open parking lot, watching bullets skip along my path as I ran.

Flooded with adrenaline, all of my limbs were numb. I

kept my head lowered and began to shuffle my feet in a zig-zag pattern, making my body a more challenging target to hit. I took notice of a round that hit close to my right foot, then, a loud thought came to me: *Ricky, make sure to guard your head!*

It was strange and surreal, but I tried to shield my head as best as possible while running—heeding my own internal warning. But I also thought of my head. If I was going to get hit, I *wanted* to feel it. If I felt it, that would mean it wasn't immediately lights out for me. Death wouldn't be inevitable—I could keep fighting.

Relief washed over me as I neared the tall privacy fence at the edge of the parking lot. I rounded the corner of the barricade, hoping it would provide extra cover. I kept running until the bullets exploding beside me stopped, then I stole a quick glance over my shoulder and realized I was clear of Mack.

My eyes locked on a Brian's car parked around fifty yards away from me.

Finally in the clear, I began to triage myself and lifted my shirt, scanning all the important places of my body for bullet holes: chest, stomach, and, of course, my crotch. Finding none, I looked up at Brian, thinking how lucky I'd gotten. I'd somehow stared down the barrel of a rifle held five yards away and never got hit.

As with every other close call in my undercover work, I came out unscathed. And just like the others, I pushed fear aside and was ready to get in the car, get a weapon, and get back in the fight. I had no clue what was happening, where Mike and Patrick were, and more importantly, where the fuck

Mack was. Nothing was clicking the way it should have. Everything swirled.

The only place on my body that still stung was my right calf. When I looked down to observe it, I realized I had just a small stream of blood leaking from two holes, which began to stain the top of my sock and shoe.

"I'm good, dude!" I called out to Brian proudly through the closed car door.

I knew the fight wasn't over, so I took a step with my left leg to get to the car and prepare for the counterassault, then was shaken as my limb collapsed beneath my weight, causing me to fall to the ground.

What the fuck? I wondered.

I pulled up my baggy shorts up and all I saw was blood. Everywhere. I struggled to my feet, then attempted to get a better look at my leg. Due to the baggy shorts that I was wearing, I couldn't see anything above my calves. It was then I realized that I'd had such tunnel vision on my right leg, I hadn't stopped to consider my left. Upon further inspection, I realized my entire left thigh was soaked in blood. When I'd tripped, trying to get behind Mike's car, I'd taken a direct hit to the back of my knee. My knee had been ripped wide open by a bullet . . . and I hadn't even felt it—and still didn't.

"COME ON!" Brian yelled. "Get in the fucking car, Ricky! Let's go!"

Horrified that I was shot, a lump formed in my throat, and I had an odd sense of embarrassment.

"Brian," I blared in a calm but serious tone as it finally hit me, "I'm shot!"

I'd just run seventy-five yards to escape gunfire, but my

leg had decided it couldn't go another step. I would have to hobble the last stretch on my right leg to get to Brian's car. Once there, I would get a better look at my left knee.

The bullet hole that went all the way through my left kneecap was almost unbearable to look at. I really couldn't even tell what was shot and what wasn't. Blood and flaps of skin were hanging from all sides of my knee. Brian and I had no tourniquet nearby, so I took my pant leg, lifted it just above my knee, and twisted the fabric as tightly as I could into a knot, putting pressure on the wound. While Brian rushed me to the hospital, I noticed that I had a good amount of blood on my left arm and hands, but I paid no attention to it. My blood was pooling on the floor, and I figured it was just from my knee, which I continued to press my bloody palms against with as much force as I could muster.

Meanwhile, Brian announced on the radio that we were officially out of the operation, as he was taking me to the hospital. We started driving west on the highway, which would take us past the parking lot I'd just escaped. Shock reverberated through my body as I watched Mack's blue Acura pull out of the Sky-Vu lot and onto the highway in front of us, traveling in the same direction we were headed—still in no hurry to escape. I begged Brian to give me his gun and pull alongside him, determined to execute him. Wisely, Brian ignored my pleas. Brian told the guys over the radio that we could not follow Mack, urging additional surveillance detectives to follow the Acura.

"You drive. Let me work the radio, man," I told Brian, taking the radio from him to broadcast future updates so he could focus on the road. This was one of the first times, but not the last, that I grabbed at anything to gain back control and avoid vulnerability. I leaned back in my seat and watched my left arm involuntarily slip on the center console, now completely soaked in blood. When I examined my arm more carefully than before, I noticed an entrance wound just above my wrist that traveled up my forearm and exited in two places near my elbow.

"Brian," I began, "I'm good, dude, but I've been hit several times."

I then took the sleeve of my shirt and fashioned another makeshift tourniquet to apply pressure just above my elbow, terrified that we wouldn't get to the hospital before I'd lost too much blood. I couldn't help but question how I'd somehow overlooked such a severe, gaping wound. No matter how much pressure I tried to apply, my arm just kept dumping blood. Soon, my seat and clothes were soaked in it.

CHAPTER 16
A LITTLE BIT OF OXYGEN

We raced to the hospital as quickly as Brian's car would allow, listening to the radio as the detectives reported in during their attempts to catch Mack—he had ditched his car and run across six lanes of Interstate 70 with his rifle in hand. Meanwhile, Brian was swerving around cars like crazy, trying not to cause a wreck. My distress was amplified when I heard Mike report over the radio he had been shot a few times. I felt overcome with guilt at the thought that I was to blame for how fucked this situation had become.

This was supposed to be a surveillance-only mission, I thought. *Worst of all, Mike and Patrick wouldn't have been there if it hadn't been for me.* I hated myself for calling an audible, for making Mike and Patrick come into the parking lot shorthanded, and then interjecting myself into their stop.

I also felt terrible for distracting Mike while we were by the police SUV, reasoning that if I hadn't been there, he would have been able to follow his usual protocol and would have likely not gotten hit, or at least shot Mack before any bullets tore through either of us. I hated myself most because, despite our efforts, Mack had escaped and was now running loose with a rifle in his hands. He clearly knew we were after him, and he was obviously going to shoot it out with whomever confronted him next. I feared that if anyone else got hurt because of Mack, I would have a hard time not internalizing it.

Perception is a bitch. When you're in a hurry, everything always seems to slow down. The emotion of the situation altered my perception of the traffic as Brian did his best to get around the other drivers on the road who were oblivious to my condition. I tried to assist as best I could by using his radio. I changed the channel to the zone we were heading into—the region of Kansas City where the hospital was located. I put out requests to any available police cars to begin blocking intersections and also requested a police car to escort us to the emergency room.

Immediately, several officers answered, and it hit me hard when I realized they were all officers I'd worked with years ago. It was clear they recognized my voice and wanted to help me, which set emotions loose in me that I wasn't used to feeling. I knew how I'd have felt if the roles were reversed and one of my teammates were rushing to the hospital riddled with bullet holes. I swallowed hard and tried to keep myself together.

The sound of sirens began to wail from every nearby block, though Brian and I didn't directly see any red and blue lights. Brian had cleared most of the traffic and we were making progress. Once we were only a few minutes away from the hospital, I requested the dispatcher to notify the ER that we "had one officer on the way with multiple gunshot wounds." My hope was to prepare the medical staff so they could treat my injuries as quickly as possible.

I directed Brian to take the back way to the hospital, as the route to the front consisted of one-way streets, which could take several minutes to navigate. We picked up one patrol car along the way, then slammed the car in park in front of the emergency room door.

We were met by a security guard who barked at Brian, demanding we move our car away from the ER entrance. It became obvious to me that the guard hadn't been notified that we were coming in, which I found infuriating, given my previous attempt to update the hospital. Brian ignored the guard, then demanded, "Open the door to the back entrance of the ER immediately."

Because the back entrance was typically used by ambulance crews and led right to the trauma rooms, the guard immediately grasped the gravity of the situation, then snapped to action. While he opened the back entrance, Brian rounded my side of the car, opened the door and looked at me, confused. I rolled out of the car and Brian tried to find somewhere to grab onto me to help, but with so much blood, he didn't know where to grab without causing more harm or pain.

I shrugged Brian off, determined to show my toughness and walk on my own, grasping onto my last shred of control to avoid vulnerability. Brian looked at me with confusion—he was powerless as I limped toward the trauma room. I pulled the door open, then let myself in, only to be met with total silence; no doctors or nurses were there to meet me. I knew the standard procedure for addressing a gunshot wound because I'd been in this very room over a hundred times as a street cop, responding to calls that then turned out to be people shot who, on many occasions, never made it out alive. I emptied my pockets and mechanically left my phone and wallet for Brian to hold.

I knew if I didn't take my clothes off on my own, the medical team would cut them off of me. I happened to be wearing my favorite undercover "Ricky" clothes, and my heart broke to think of them getting ruined as a team of doctors peeled them off of my bloody trunk and wounded limbs. Stripped down to my boxers, I sat on the trauma bed, holding pressure on my leg. Finally, I was able to see a better view of the damage: on the outside of my left knee, I had a hole about the size of a tennis ball. A large flap of skin was hanging down that looked like a peeled banana. On the inside of my left knee were two quarter-sized holes, and my kneecap was drooping outward, far out of place. I had an odd sense of calm as I looked at this, clearly out of touch with everything that had happened.

Brian and I were put into an odd situation as we sat unattended for a few minutes inside the trauma room. These rooms were at the end of a secluded hallway, and Brian remained calm as he tried to locate someone to help me. As I continued to mitigate blood loss, I bitched about the doctors taking too long, not recognizing the full extent of what I'd just lived through. It took mere seconds, and a flood of nurses and doctors rushed in and began treating my injuries. The quiet room was now abuzz with conversations: physicians and medical students asking me questions all at once.

"You were super gracious to get undressed for us," one of the female doctors joked.

"Sure," I began, "and I was also gracious enough to leave my underwear on so Brian wouldn't get jealous."

I waited for anyone to laugh, but my joke fell flat. My tendency to use humor to push this sort of shit aside was definitely not going to work. This was the first time I would receive the appropriate reaction to my jokes after something dangerous occurred, and I actually took notice.

The lead doctor asked in a calm voice what happened to me.

"I'm an undercover cop, and some asshole shot me," I said.

"Where are you shot?" the doctor questioned.

I began showing her each injury from smallest to largest. As she swept my body for wounds, she detailed every necessary bit of information for the medical students who were in attendance.

"Gunshot wounds can be hidden and tricky; this is why we'll want to check him over fully," she concluded.

The doctor scanned me from head to toe, intermittently yelling out medical terms that a nearby nurse proceeded to document. I tried to take control, speaking over them to tell Brian what to do with my clothes and where to put my phone and wallet so they wouldn't be taken in as evidence. After answering each of the doctor's questions, I went back to telling Brian how to unlock my phone, who to call to get ahold of Wesley, and exactly what he should say. Once the doctor was finished with the exam of my front side, her team rolled me onto my stomach to inspect my back.

The moment she rolled me over, her next words sent me into an immediate spiral of terror.

"See, this is why we don't take their word for it; we have another one back here."

Another? I panicked.

If there's one in the back that doesn't have an exit wound in the front, then that means . . . the bullet released all of its energy into my core and, potentially, passing through my organs.

I froze in fear, trying to control my breathing.

Fuck. Fuck. Fuck. This is bad. This is very bad.

Wounds like this are how people die—if my insides took the full brunt of a bullet, it likely turned my surrounding tissue to mush, I reasoned. *I'm dead. I am going to die today.*

I can't believe I'm going to fucking die.

Once again, my world slowed down, just as it had while Mack's bullets had been flying at me. Though the noise of the room continued to roar around me, I could hear nothing but the sound of my heart pounding.

I was in such a daze that I was unable to hear the doctor tell the tracking nurse the location of the additional bullet wound. I laid on the table, certain I was dying, for what felt like hours.

I finally returned to the present moment when the doctor asked if anyone else had been with me.

"My buddy Mike will be coming in," I told her. "He's shot. I'm not sure how bad, but he's been hit several times."

The surrounding nurses darted off to prepare a bed for Mike to lie in, adjacent to mine.

Only when the doctors started to pay less attention to me did I finally look up at Brian and ask, "Where did they say I got hit? I didn't hear a goddamn thing."

"Your left triceps," he said, patting my right shoulder. The round had skipped from the pavement and sheared in half. As the round entered my left triceps, it had tumbled, creating a large wound. Ultimately, the round broke my humerus and came to rest. This made sense. I'd tied my tourniquet below the bullet wound to stop the bleeding from the exit wounds in my elbow. Doing that had caused all the pumping and pooling blood to flow out of that wound and all over me and my seat.

I guffawed with relief, even amused that they'd barely cleaned my wounds before sending me off to get an X-ray to ensure there was no further damage. As they began wheeling me out of the trauma room, Brian stopped me. He told me he couldn't find my old boss Deb's phone number, so he was going to call Wesley instead.

"Bad idea, man, bad idea," I said, chuckling, knowing it would send Wesley into a spiral. "You have to call Deb. She knows my wife well. She should be the one to relay the news." I gave Brian my passcode again, then was wheeled behind the closed doors of the X-ray room.

The X-ray room was cold, dark, and quiet. Just like all the others I'd been in. As the technician prepared the machine, all I could do was attempt to piece together what the fuck had just happened to me. Now in silence and all alone, tears welled in my eyes, then began to flow uncontrollably. As a result, my breathing slowed, which inevitably triggered the alarm on the oxygen sensor.

"You all right? You breathing?" the nurse called out.

"Yeah," I answered, my face now covered in wet, gleaming tear streaks.

"Take some deep breaths," she said. "We've got to raise your oxygen levels."

There, in the quiet dark, my traumatized brain began to reconcile my brush with death. And for the first time since the evolution of Ricky, the real and total version of Brent Cartwright returned.

CHAPTER 17
PRIMAL PANIC

When I was wheeled out of the X-ray room, I was met by Brian with a worried expression on his face. "Look, man," he began, "I decided to go ahead and call your wife and . . . it DID NOT go well."

This made me laugh harder than it should have, given that Wesley was probably losing her mind by that point. "I told you so. You shouldn't have done that!" I exclaimed, still chuckling. Brian didn't laugh in response. This made me sure something else was wrong.

"What is it?" I asked.

"Shit's not over. There was a big shootout and Buck got hit." My body, which was already in a pretty fucked-up state, went cold as Brian said this. Buck was a detective in our Career Criminal Squad. He'd come in to help track Mack down, as did hundreds of officers like him, after Mike and I got shot—another teammate put on the scene to catch Mack because of my arrest plan.

"I don't know how bad," he continued, "but . . . it doesn't sound good."

Guilt weighed so heavily upon my body that I could hardly sit upright.

First Mike, now Buck, I agonized.

As I ruminated on the news, the ER physicians placed me in a temporary room until a proper hospital bed could be made available to me. Once there, a nurse came to clean my wounds further and rinse the bullet channels with saline.

"Bear with me; this is going to be painful," the nurse said.

I invited it as a penalty. I sat quietly, resisting the urge to flinch, enduring the pain.

Once the nurse was done, he assured me he would be placing me in a hospital room as soon as possible. I asked him if they were going to wrap or stitch up my wounds. He informed me that wouldn't be done, as it could cause an infection, meaning I would spend at least the next few hours staring at my exploded knee and the morbid bullet holes that marked my flesh. During this time, I ruminated on how the scene Ricky created caused Brent, in all his completeness of emotion and registration of experiences, back to the surface.

It didn't help my case that I was still being transferred in the same bed where the X-ray tech had examined me. When the nurses moved me from the trauma bed to the new mobile bed, I realized I'd been lying on a pile of blood-soaked sheets, with shredded muscles, white tendons, and glaring bullet holes on display for all the world to see.

Now everyone will know what I look like on the inside, I thought, and this terrified me.

From my temporary room, I could see crowds of people walking by, heading to what I knew was Mike's room. I couldn't help but feel a little on display as people slowed down to poke their heads into my door, my carnage exposed—inciting both disgust and intrigue in passersby.

For whatever reason, others gawking at me made me burn with shame—like they were seeing past all of my exteriors: both Ricky's and Brent's.

I wonder if all of them know I'm the reason Mike and Buck were shot, I'd think, anguish gnawing at the insides of my stomach. I dreaded facing my wife, close friends, and coworkers—all of whom were on their way and, realistically, probably just relieved that I'd survived.

Within an hour, ten people were standing in my room, and I was sitting there—laughing and joking like the asshole I am, just trying to lighten the mood. I tried so hard to get everyone around me laughing that I started physically shaking—my body rejecting my attempt to override and play it cool after enduring the hell of that vicious assault. This was my sign, and I knew it—I would no longer be able to suppress the previous psychological and physical tortures that Ricky had inflicted upon my body. Once I left the hospital, I would have to choose—Ricky or Brent. Only one of us could stay. I could barely think about it, so I pushed the thought out of my mind.

As I continued shaking, the nurse called to get me a blanket, believing I was cold, then realized it was probably a bad idea to cover the wounds.

"Your wounds are going to have to breathe for a bit," the nurse stated.

At about that time, Wesley rounded the corner to my room, a look of pure fear on her face that made me surmise she'd not been told that I was going to live.

"Wes, I'm fine, babe," I began, watching her eyes drift to the hole in my knee.

Immediately, her expression contorted into one of terror, her speech began to slur, then, with one gasping breath, she collapsed to the floor in the throes of a terrible panic attack. Watching my wife being ushered out of the room in a wheelchair, wearing an oxygen mask, made my mind race.

Another person I love is hurt because of me.

My family deserves better.

I could only imagine that Mike's wife and Buck's wife were in the same position. All I could do was sit there, feeling like I was at fault. However, the people in my room were relieved that I was okay; the concerned looks on their faces let me know that they genuinely cared for my well-being. In some ways, this made my self-loathing even worse. I determined that since these people would not punish me, it was my responsibility to punish myself.

A few hours later, I received an update about the entire situation. From a perch inside an abandoned house, Mack had rained down rounds on dozens of officers for over an hour. It seemed he was running low on ammunition, so he'd kicked down the rear door and raced outside. As he ran out of the house, he furiously fired at every officer on the perimeter, trying to take out as many men and women as possible. His erratic gunfire never landed on a target.

Every officer stayed calm under fire, firing several perfectly placed rounds that brought him down. Once Mack was down, they jumped into action in a tug of war of emotions. The man who had shot three of their brothers and tried to kill them now lay motionless. After being forced to shoot someone, officers are required to provide life-saving treatment until medical personnel can arrive. So, my teammates ran across the open landscape, disarmed Mack, and began CPR. Despite the immediate first aid, Mack did not survive the day.

As the hours ticked by, the nurses and doctors came in several times to check on me, offering me medication to ease my suffering. Every time—I declined.

You need to hurt. Ricky needs to hurt the way Mike and Buck hurt.

There was no other way in my mind to pay penance but to deny myself painkillers. Hour by hour, I abandoned myself to a sea of physiological torture.

Late in the evening, I was visited by an orthopedic surgeon who informed me that he wasn't sure if he would be doing surgery to repair my wounds. I'd had a misconception —born from watching too much television—that doctors always remove bullets. Turns out that's not the case in the real world. The doctor talked to me about the damage of my bullet wounds, focusing primarily on my knee. He told me that not only did he not feel comfortable doing surgery on my knee, but that my running days were over.

I felt debilitated by this news.

Like many officers, running was about my only source of exercise—my embraced form of cardio for almost thirty years. And just like that, it was gone. The surgeon proceeded to evade all questions about how my leg would function moving forward.

"I can't speak to that as this is beyond my level of expertise," he admitted. "I'm going to have to refer you to a different surgeon."

When I spoke with the second surgeon around midnight, he seemed upbeat about my ability to recover but was worried about the complexity of my injury.

The bullets to my knee had shattered dozens of pieces of bone as they zipped through me: some small, others larger. The goal during the surgery would be to repair damage to my tendons and cartilage and clear out the bullet and bone fragments inside my joint. Everything else would stay.

While the surgeons deliberated over whether to repair my knee or not, I was put on food restriction, just in case they had to do surgery. To make matters worse, the room across the hall was the setup point for all food donations for visiting officers, doctors, and nurses. I kept watching groups gather, chatting and laughing as they enjoyed a buffet of food; honestly, the longer I lay there, the more it pissed me off. I knew I wouldn't run again, but I also feared I might not walk again. I was terrified, and the people in the next room were just steps away, having a totally different emotional experience than me. An hour later, my new surgeon came in and explained that he would attempt to piece my knee back together the following day.

"Bullets and fragments migrate to all places in your body; the only ones worth going after are the ones that can move into a joint," he informed me. He went on to explain that he intended to remove only the bare minimum of metal from my knee, leaving the remaining bullets and fragments untouched.

"So, I guess July 15th is going to be a part of me forever, isn't it?" I asked.

"I think so, unfortunately—but you'd be amazed at how our bodies can heal around bullets," the surgeon assured me.

That evening, I was starving and watching people chowing across the hall. They'd pop in and say, "How you doing?"

I'd think to myself, *Fuck off.* But I'd say, "Good," in an aggressive tone and leave it at that.

I just wanted to be left alone. Anger is a great cover for more vulnerable emotions such as shame or fear. And for me, shame had set in hard.

In truth, I don't know why I did what I did on July 15th. The decision to run up to Mike wasn't a fully conscious one. As I stayed awake day and night, I could never find the "aha" moment that explained my actions.

My surgery was scheduled for my second afternoon in the hospital. After surgery, once I came down from the anesthesia, I crashed. I'd totally lost my drive to put on a happy face for people. The somewhat upbeat façade I'd displayed the first twenty-four hours was gone. Depression was setting in, and my morphine regimen did nothing but make it easier to stake my claim in the heaviness.

I had restricted all visitors to just my family and spent my waking hours trying to figure out just what in the hell had happened. I started talking to my family incessantly, trying to make sense of how that day unfolded—all the parts that still felt fragmented—and I began to realize that my memory was "off" about the details of July 15th.

My physical therapist would come in and get me walking just a few hours after surgery. At one point during our work together, I migrated toward Mike's room. His space was a much different scene. Before catching a glimpse through the open door, I could already hear the roar of people's laughter. His space didn't feel glum, like my room. Probably because he didn't restrict all visitors like I did.

I made it through the doorway with the help of my physical therapist and immediately felt the urge to thank Mike for saving me that day. I wasn't sure how to word it, though, because I'd essentially just cowered behind his body and car.

"Mike, I'm so sorry, dude," I finally choked out. At which point, he gave me a wave of his hand, passing me off, as I proceeded to talk about my recollections of that day. I tried to explain myself, talking in circles, even trying to find my own justification. As I concluded, I noticed the expressions of several people in the room twisting into confusion. However, I was too overloaded with emotion to stop and ask why they were responding this way. It wasn't until weeks later that I learned *why* Mike stopped me mid-story to say, "Dude, we won. We're alive and he's fucking dead," before changing the subject.

Without any further discussion about July 15th, I returned to my room and devolved into my own personal pity party. I didn't buy Mike's kind disposition toward me. The only thing I could do was proceed to punish myself once again by refusing pain medicine. This time would be problematic, though, because I'd taken them the day of my surgery, meaning my body was already primed for a reaction. My refusal to take another dose left me vomiting and curled up in a ball in pain from withdrawals: *the pain I deserved for all that I'd done.*

This pain was only tempered by the news that Buck had been released. He was lucky to be alive, as the round that tore his bicep apart had ricocheted off the front sight post of his AR while he exchanged fire with Mack. Had that bullet been a half-inch either way, Buck would've been dead. It was later brought up that Mike would be leaving the hospital soon, while my injuries would keep me in the hospital for a few extra days.

That's what you fucking get, moron.

Once the guys were gone, I fell into a deeper depression.

Two more days dragged by at the hospital, and the foot traffic that was once prevalent decreased significantly. My family and a few friends were the only ones who stopped by, aside from my ATF supervisor, Eric. In between these visitors, I slept pretty well, despite how much pain I was in. The nurse came into my room and told me I was leaving at some point in the afternoon.

From the moment I'd hobbled into the hospital, all I'd wanted was to leave. Now, it would be time to walk out. The thought sent nerves firing through my body, much like the feelings I had during my first undercover buy as Ricky.

It felt like I was about to enter a strange, new world—and I was. My life and the world around me had changed. Everything was foreign to me. When I was finally escorted out of the north entrance of the hospital to my dad's car, the only people who were there were my parents, wife, and Eric. Life was simple again. I took in the hot afternoon sun and looked around at the one area of Kansas City I knew best but didn't recognize; it felt like I was living in a dream world.

Once home, I asked to be left alone, feeling out of it. All I'd wanted at the hospital was to be home, but home felt strange, and I was crawling out of my skin. Mentally, I was far from being present. All I could do was sit down on my couch and look around—staring and weeping. I cried constantly. I think it was because I knew my days of numbing out and doing what no one else could or would do were over. Plain and simple, Ricky's days were over.

I shouldn't be home, I'd think. *I should be dead.*

I wanted to run away—to leave and go anywhere, but I couldn't. Driving was not an option yet, so the only thing I could do was to try to start walking. My first walk was alone in my neighborhood on crutches, and I felt the compression in my head and lungs as I moved. All I wanted was to test the world and ensure my surroundings were real. I puzzled over what really happened on July 15th, as there were gaping holes in my memory. The only thing I could remember was that I'd wrongfully chosen to call an audible, then interject myself into an arrest, and Mike, Buck, and I almost died because of it.

Tortured by blaming myself for something I couldn't fully recall, I finally broke down and called Riley, who had been on the other end of the phone while I was at Sky-Vu. I needed to know what other people were saying about that day, and he was the only person that wouldn't throw some sugarcoated bullshit my way.

However, when I called, Riley surprised me by completely deflecting my questions. Amped up on anxiety, it didn't take me long to launch back into telling the story as I remembered it. He didn't correct me or say much at all, so my anxiety transitioned to rage. I was angry at my department for switching my phone to that shitty carrier, blaming them for the dropped calls that gave Mack time to get to his car and delayed Mike. I was pissed at myself for being a distraction. And I was just plain mad at everything I knew I was going to lose with my new physical limitations. By the time I hung up the phone, I was slobbering from the mouth, my face was wet with tears, and my heart was racing.

I made my way into the house and walked into the bathroom to take a piss. As I struggled to navigate with crutches, my frustrations only grew. My heart pounded as I stared into the wall and peed, noticing small circles of color appearing in my vision. Within seconds, I collapsed to the floor.

Heart still pounding, my vision went technicolor as I sensed the unmistakable taste of burnt gunpowder in my mouth. The taste was exactly as it had been when I was standing in front of Mack. The AK-47 he was firing had such a short barrel that much of the gunpowder was unburned, causing fire and gunpowder to spew toward Mike and me. I lay there with my dick in my hand and the percussion of an assault rifle ringing in my ears. The bright flashes in my eyes, the pressure slamming my chest, and the taste of gunpowder all put me right back into the Sky-Vu parking lot.

Had I not been in my bathroom, I would have been

certain someone was shooting at me. The only reason I knew it wasn't gunfire was that I could make out the decorative turkey tail fan hanging on the wall of the 3x5 ft room. Though I knew I wasn't being fired upon, that didn't stop my mind from pushing me into full-on panic mode.

Vertigo took hold of me, and my flashing vision almost immediately became blurry vision. I was unable to work my hands or zip up my pants. My instincts were telling me to find somewhere to hide as if my life depended on it. Yet there was no danger in my home, and I logically understood that. Still, I could not override the flashback and its inherent wave of visceral fear that causes one to question just exactly what reality is. It was as real as any life-or-death struggle I'd ever endured. It was pure panic.

For the better part of an hour, I felt like a soldier dodging bombs in a foxhole. When I was finally able to pull myself from the floor, things were different. I pulled myself up with sheer willpower, still on high alert, as if someone might attack me at any moment. It was here that an overwhelming sense of hypervigilance came to define my life. I crept into my bedroom and sat on the bed for the rest of the night: no television, no phone, just sitting and staring out the window.

Without a real understanding of what had just gone on, my wife alleviated me from all family duties that night. After she went to sleep, I stayed awake.

This is it—my first night at home. No sleep, just staring out of windows.

For weeks, my body refused to come out of high alert; the pressure never faded and only grew worse with the sleep deprivation it caused. Though I felt tired, I refused to close my eyes. If I did, I knew I'd have another flashback. I had no idea that my mind and body were stuck: fight-or-flight reflexes had kicked in, and I didn't know how to return to some kind of baseline. This primal survival instinct, which had only grown stronger with the birth and evolution of Ricky, was now working against me.

It was then that I realized if I didn't get help, I might stay in primal panic forever. If I couldn't get help to un-fuck my brain—it might cost me my life.

CHAPTER 18
RECOVERY

In early August, I learned that Mike had gotten the police footage from the day at Sky-Vu, and others were passing it around the department. By the time I returned to work in October, everyone in the squad had seen it. They'd watched Mike and me getting shot from multiple angles—were shocked at how the bullets flew and were amazed that we'd survived. When I asked to see the video, no one would send it to me.

I was called into an official debrief, where I spoke with my bosses, downplaying the impact that July 15th had on me, pleading for them to let me stay in a position that I loved.

My department-assigned therapist could clearly see my incapacity to stay focused on what was immediately happening in my environment. I'd get distracted by something as simple as the wind blowing through the trees, causing movement I couldn't predict or control. He had to repeat things over and over, just for me to retain what he was saying. I had a severe limp, and I was hammered with intrusive thoughts, hypervigilance, lack of focus, and a body that was charged with fight-or-flight energy. I hadn't slept for more than two hours a night since being shot. I was outnumbered by my terrors, and now I was outnumbered by the general consensus among my supervisors: my undercover career was over.

I was no longer Ricky.

And my transition into undercover work meant that I was no longer Brent.

I was damaged goods. So, what fucking purpose did I serve now?

I had more voids from the incident than I had actual memories of what happened, and what I did remember was unreliable.

For the few nights I managed to get more than two hours of sleep, I had nightmares. In my dreams, I would hear someone breaking into my car and storm outside to confront them. Once I grabbed them, I would get shot several times. The pain made me writhe. I felt as if I was dripping with blood, and its bitter, tinny taste filled my mouth. As I stumbled around in the dark, trying to find a hospital, I fell to the ground. The moment I was about to die, I would wake up and launch out of bed. Covered in sweat, I would look around my room and try to catch my breath.

Then, it would happen again. A loud crash would come from my driveway, and I'd hobble to my window to see a man breaking into my truck. I'd grab my gun and sneak out my side door to surprise the thief. The moment I'd get to him, he'd turn and shoot me in the stomach, then take off on a bicycle. I'd lay on the ground, dying, unable to get to my cell phone to call 911. As my eyes closed, with death slithering over my body, I'd wake up.

I was having dreams inside of dreams inside of dreams. Each time I woke up, I never knew whether I was really awake or dreaming. These dreams were so vivid; each time I woke up, I could have sworn it was real life. I felt every ounce of pain from the gunshots—there was no pinching myself to know if I was asleep or not. This became a big problem if one of my young children had a nightmare and entered the room to ask to crawl into bed with Wesley and me for comfort. The second she tapped on my shoulder, sheets soaked in sweat, I would launch out of bed feeling like I was being attacked. With my fists clenched, I'd begin swinging, trying to destroy whoever dared to get near me. Inevitably, my eyes would land on my five-year-old daughter, Blake, who had narrowly missed being struck in my panic. There was no controlling it. I'd become so messed up that I could no longer transition reliably or safely from dream to reality.

The best way to get some sleep—and ensure it was never deep enough for nightmares—was to drink, and drink heavily. There was no shortage of booze—this was how everyone bonded over the event, so bar nights took place at least five nights a week. I was warned against drinking, as it was probably the worst thing to do in my case. But it felt like the easy solution. And frankly, it worked.

As if the flashbacks and nightmares weren't bad enough, I was also intermittently having my knee evaluated by my new orthopedic surgeon, who never seemed to have good news.

After two additional surgeries, the surgeon finally sat me down and said there was nothing more that she could do. She emphasized the fact that my loss of feeling and limited motor control from my knee down was irreparable. My debilitating, shooting nerve pain would be permanent. The pain was so bad that I seriously considered amputation, but my neurologist warned me about the harsh reality of ghost pains—meaning I could still suffer from the same exact pain even without my leg. I would likely never return to duty—or at least not until I could pass the "fit-for-duty" evaluation, which didn't seem likely in the near future.

I had every intention to return to duty, regardless of my limitations. Determined, I attempted the fit-for-duty test and, just as my doctor had warned, I failed. My knee was just not stable enough to do the physical exercises. My HR department sent me for another exam with yet another "doctor." I spent twenty minutes sitting on the paper-covered chair in the exam room with a doctor who spoke slowly and asked stupid questions like, "Who mows your lawn? How many stairs are in your house?"

After this sham of an appointment, she determined I could perform the duties as outlined by whatever vague work description my department provided her, and I was cleared to come back to work—limp and all. Despite my lack of belief in the doctor's abilities, I didn't fight this. I wanted to come back and prove myself, like I always did.

I can do fucking anything.

My lingering psychological problems were a hangup, though. I was taking all kinds of medications to sleep and to keep me numb enough to survive each day. But just as HR did with my physical injuries, they found a way to clear me. Fifteen months later, I returned to full duty back in the Gun Squad. I wish I could say the department welcomed me back kindly when I got the go-ahead, but they didn't. By that point, I walked with a limp, and my hands shook constantly from a newfound inability to control my body's response to any stressors or adrenaline dumps. Where once I craved these sensations and used them to perform my job at the highest level, they were now a hindrance, ramping up my already overflowing shame.

I kept a flask filled to the brim with alcohol in my minivan for the drive home each night, as it was the only way to calm my anxiety. I pushed through for a full year. I made it through the riots of 2020 and one of the deadliest summers Kansas City has ever had. Unlike during my time as an undercover, I could now see my life finally beginning to collapse.

During this time, our squad was constantly taking down the most violent criminals in Kansas City, and I found myself repeatedly jumping out with my gun drawn. But something was off, and I couldn't shake it when I was involved in the takedowns of two particularly violent criminals.

For the first takedown, I used my van to help pin an armed robbery crew inside a parking lot. From my position, crouched behind my van, I had a clear shot of one of the suspects who pulled a gun and was trying to kill my teammates. But, as I raised my gun, I almost dropped it. My hands shook wildly, and I couldn't accurately hold my sights on my intended target. During the other incident, the trembling returned, and I felt helpless. As my entire squad held tight, guns drawn on an armed murderer, I failed in my coverage responsibility and had to back away from the scene. I could not defend myself, my partners, or the public. And I fucking knew it. I cried for a week straight, trying to decide if I could keep pushing through for ten more years, or if I should summon the courage to tell the department, "No more," and make the best decision for my family and me.

On Thanksgiving Day, I took vacation time for the first time in years. With my face buried in my hands and streaked with tears, I made a phone call to my current therapist, telling him I was at my breaking point.

"I can't do this anymore. I can't function. I'm going to get somebody killed, man," I told him.

"What took so long?" he asked. Later, I discovered that his notes stated he had expected this outcome for over a year but had refused to pull me out unless I asked.

He relieved me from duty for my mental well-being and, shortly afterwards, I was assigned a new therapist. I fought this with every ounce of my being, but with worker's compensation, I had zero say. So, I started seeing Dr. Jennifer Prohaska, a clinical psychologist in Kansas City who specializes in the worst of the worst—patients who had failed most other treatments and had life-altering physical injuries and the neuropsychological changes that came with extreme trauma. Dr. Prohaska specifically had experience working with individuals like me—those who had dedicated their lives to public safety and then suffered serious injuries in the line of duty.

Lacking control over my choice of doctor, I entered the relationship Dr. Prohaska carrying a severe chip on my shoulder—an attitude that put her at an extreme disadvantage in her efforts to help me heal. I had a previous interaction with her early on in my recovery, and to be nice about it, I fucking hated her. I didn't trust her; I saw her as part of the system designed to fuck me over. I told her just as much, beginning our first conversation with a long list of why I couldn't stand her and how I was against this forced relationship.

Then, I added one caveat: "But I don't give a fuck about all that. I just want to get better." I hung my head. "I'm tired of being broken."

It took several months before I really surrendered and gave in to the entire process, but I meant what I said that day. In that moment, I recognized that nobody could heal for me. I had to *want* to get better, and I did, although it took me a while to understand that it was possible. The trauma and suffering I'd experienced during my time as Ricky was so vast that it seemed to eclipse Brent entirely. I couldn't wrap my head around the idea that I would ever recover from it—that I would ever hear a gunshot, hold a gun, or even smell a joint without the painful memories flooding back to me. My years of living on pure adrenaline and burying every serious event had put me in a dark place.

But I knew remaining in that dark place would ruin my life—I wanted to be the husband, father, and man my family deserved. Dr. Prohaska brought an aggressive and very direct approach, but one that had a purpose. She was blunt with me: "You will never fully heal from what you endured during your time as a cop, specifically as an undercover." She made me realize that I was a product of a skewed culture that sought to bury this shit down and hide from problems like they were a sign of weakness.

It would take several years for me to see—and actually *believe*—that getting shot was what saved my life. Had I not been shot on that Sunday in July 2015, I have no doubt that I would've kept progressing into a downward spiral, which would have ultimately led to my death. The risks I was willing to take would have finally caught up with me. My eventual recognition of this initially set me down the wrong course, and those dark years are full of many regrets. My family suffered alongside me, just in a different way. They always did, whether I was working or injured.

I was retired from duty from the Kansas City Missouri Police Department, not for my physical injuries but for my mental ones. There was a time when I was ashamed of this, due to the stigma that mental health carries. But shame can only live in the dark, and I openly discuss this to break this misconception. Every person has a breaking point for what they can endure mentally and physically. I just happened to find mine and attempted to ignore it as I always had, and found out the hard way it was not only impossible, but it had the potential to create even more problems.

Today, I have a clearer sense of self and purpose in my life—one that isn't defined as the junkie I once was. This life of Ricky is one that I own and am proud of. I am fortunate to be

Brent Cartwright again, though a muted version of Ricky will always live within me.

ABOUT THE AUTHOR

Retired Detective Brent Cartwright dedicated over 25 years to serving as a U.S. Army veteran and police officer, spending more than a decade as an undercover detective. He is the recipient of numerous awards and decorations, including the Purple Heart and a Commendation for Valor. Cartwright is recognized by the U.S. Criminal Courts as an expert witness in narcotics trafficking and illegal firearms crimes. *Undercover Junkie* is his first book.

www.ingramcontent.com/pod-product-compliance
Lightning Source LLC
LaVergne TN
LVHW051938280125
802395LV00001B/1/J